Family Science Night

Fun Tips, Activities, and Ideas

Shelley Connell, Ed.D.

Routledge
Taylor & Francis Group
New York London

First published 2013 by Eye On Education

Published 2013 by Routledge
711 Third Avenue, New York, NY 10017, USA
2 Park Square, Milton Park, Abingdon, Oxon OX14 4RN

Routledge is an imprint of the Taylor & Francis Group, an informa business

Cover Designer: Dave Strauss, 3FoldDesign

Library of Congress Cataloging-in-Publication Data

Connell, Shelley.
Family science night / Shelley Connell.
p. cm.
Includes index.
ISBN 978-1-59667-222-2
1. Science--Study and teaching (Elementary)--Activity programs. 2. Education--Parent participation. 3. Family recreation. I. Title.
LB1585.C664 2012
372.35′044--dc23 2012023123

ISBN: 978-1-596-67222-2 (pbk)

Also Available from Eye On Education

Family Math Night:
Math Standards in Action
Jennifer Taylor-Cox

Family Math Night:
Middle School Math Standards in Action
Jennifer Taylor-Cox and Christine Oberdorf

Family Reading Night
Darcy J. Hutchins, Marsha D. Greenfeld, Joyce L. Epstein

Multicultural Partnerships:
Involve All Families
Darcy J. Hutchins, Marsha D. Greenfeld, Joyce L. Epstein,
Mavis G. Sanders, and Claudia L. Galindo

Write with Me:
Partnering with Parents in Writing Instruction
Lynda Wade Sentz

Math in Plain English:
Literacy Strategies for the Mathematics Classroom
Amy Benjamin

Differentiating Assessment in Middle and High School Mathematics and Science
Sheryn Spencer Waterman

Differentiated Instruction for K–8 Math and Science:
Ideas, Activities, and Lesson Plans
Mary Hamm and Dennis Adams

Assessing Middle and High School Mathematics and Science:
Differentiating Formative Assessment
Sheryn Spencer Waterman

Teaching, Learning, and Assessment Together:
Reflective Assessments for Middle and High School Mathematics and Science
Arthur K. Ellis and David W. Denton

Solving Behavior Problems in Math Class:
Academic, Learning, Social, and Emotional Empowerment (Grades K–12)
Jennifer Taylor-Cox

Dedication

Sheldon, you are the epitome of encouragement—thank you for dreaming with me. Jordy, SJ, and Shakira—this book is for you. Thank you, Mom and Dad, for igniting my passion for science. Chet, Quita, CJ, and Zachary—thank you for your unending support. Jefferson School PTA and Roxbury School District—you will always be my Family Science Night home. To the 18 "smart cookies" of 2GC/Room 8—you are permanently in my heart. Kailen and Jamira—remember to dream big. Thank you, God, for the chance to connect two great loves—families and science.

A very special thank you to the best editor I could ask for. Thanks, Lauren!

This book is also dedicated to the memory of Scott Huguenin, who faithfully supported Family Science Night at Jefferson School year after year. His inspiration and love for science has sparked an eternal flame that will forever live in the hearts of those who knew him.

About the Author

Shelley S. Connell, Ed.D., received her bachelor's degree from the University of Maryland Eastern Shore, earned a master's degree and a doctorate at Morgan State University, and holds teaching certificates from Texas and New Jersey. It was in the classroom that she found a love for merging her two passions—education and science, having first been employed as a laboratory scientist in Maryland. She has since authored peer-reviewed articles in science and education, evaluated a major mathematics and reading intervention program in the U.S. Virgin Islands schools, worked as an adjunct faculty member for Nova Southeastern University, and been a committed board member for her local PTA. Today, Shelley is a classroom teacher, provides science enrichment for school districts, continues to serve as an adjunct faculty member for Nova Southeastern, and is working on a science fiction series for children. As a teacher in both formal and informal classroom settings, she is passionate about building a strong connection with parents to empower their children to succeed in any subject area.

Shelley currently lives in northern New Jersey with her husband of 11 years, two energetic children, and her dog, Blossom. She loves to travel with her family, read fantastic books, bake delicious desserts and breakfast foods, and stay active in her church. She is always on the lookout for new and exciting twists on scientific investigations.

Contents

Prologue

When I was a little girl, my dad said, "Choose math or science, and you'll go far, Shelley." So, I lived and breathed science (partly because I couldn't seem to earn more than a B– or C+ in math!). From candy-striping to taking college-prep courses to engaging in hospital-based internships, I did everything I could to understand scientific principles. My mom sealed my passion for science by giving me a vote of confidence every time I joined a new science venture.

As I grew older, though, the advanced science courses I took in high school and later in college became increasingly difficult. I remember crying during my first semester in college because I couldn't seem to earn the B that was required to keep my honors' scholarship (which was important because it included townhouse-style living and a full meal plan). I was devastated. How could something I loved so much cause me so much grief?

At the end of that first semester, I was placed on academic probation, and part of my scholarship was temporarily revoked. The experience of struggling through science courses became the impetus for my passion to discover ways to make scientific concepts simple enough for anyone to understand—starting with me. I found ways to "dissect" scientific principles into bite-size chunks I could understand. By my sophomore year in college, I was earning perfect scores on botany exams and Bs on chemistry exams. My efforts to dissect the principles into manageable chunks worked . . . and I felt great!

I decided to funnel this passion for dissecting scientific principles into a career as a science writer. But as it turns out, I discovered a door to pursuing a doctorate in science education instead. After just one year in the program, I became hooked on effectively communicating science as an educator rather than as a writer. From there I began to lead and develop a series of informal learning programs in science for students in grades preK through 8 and later became a full-time science educator.

I have my husband to thank for supporting my childhood dream of pursuing science as I settled into my career as an adult. Earning a doctorate in science education is not easy; he was my moral support every step of the way.

I share my love for science everywhere I go, so much that everyone who knows me is familiar with my passion for it. It even carried over to the PTA meetings I attended as a board member. Eventually, the PTA asked if I would be interested in adding a new theme to their already existing family fun night programs. What do you think I said when I was asked to bring a portable science laboratory for 100 eager elementary children and their families to explore? YES!

In short, my journey to Family Science Nights started with a lot of pep talks from my dad, votes of confidence from my mom, a couple of nearly disastrous courses, support from my husband, time spent coordinating and teaching a number of science programs, and a window of opportunity in my local school district. I now host Family Science Nights at all the elementary schools in my district and have begun to expand to surrounding districts. I bring my passion for science, my experience in effectively communicating scientific principles, and nearly 15 years in formal and informal education to you in an easy-to-follow format. This book is conveniently broken down into two sections: Getting Started (finding funding, forming a planning committee, getting volunteers, buying and storing materials, and setting up stations) and the Action Toolkit (22 reproducible station activities and illustrations, supply lists, and setup instructions for each station). My hope is that you will be inspired to create opportunities for families to explore hands-on investigations together and to cultivate positive attitudes toward science!

Introduction: Benefits of Family Science Nights

> Science Night is a prime example of the power that exists when the school and the homes join forces. ... It is also compelling evidence of [the] assertion that learning and fun are not mutually exclusive; in fact, they should go hand-in-hand. (Condon, 2011)

This quote that the principal of my daughter's school gave a local newspaper captures the essence of why Family Science Nights are great. It reveals the amazing, lifelong memories that students, families, teachers, and administrators can create when working together to participate in a Family Science Night.

Why Family Science Night?

Because of budget cuts and competing time to focus on mathematics and reading in school, hands-on science often gets the short end of the stick in K–12 education. Family Science Nights are a wonderful way to start taking up any slack. They cultivate creativity, imagination, and innovation when the stations are simple, are easy to follow, and are presented in a discovery format of open-ended questions. These types of activities can lead to at least four benefits:

- self-initiated science discovery at home
- positive attitudes toward science for students and parents
- increased understanding by parents of the science standards
- greater scientific literacy

Tip:

The primary goals of a Family Science Night should be short and simple. Here are two simple goals for a fun and meaningful event:

1. Align hands-on activities with science standards.
2. Create an atmosphere of meaningful parent involvement.

What the Research Says about the Benefits of Family Science Nights

> Sixty-five percent of scientists and science graduate students say their interest in science began before middle school, according to a study in the March 2010 *International Journal of Science Education.* Women were more likely to report that their interest was sparked by school-related activities, and most men said trying experiments at home and reading science fiction inspired them. (Stainburn, 2011. Reprinted with permission of Hechinger Institute.)

In a 2010 study on parent involvement, researchers Walker, Shenker, and Hoover-Dempsey suggested family fun nights as a venue to facilitate whole-family participation. Their specific recommendation was for school personnel to "organize family-centric activities to bring parents and students to the school to play together (e.g., family fun nights, swim night . . .)." What better event for parents and children to "play together" than at a fun Family Science Night?

A Vignette

A friend of mine, Sandra, once shared the following sentiments with me in an e-mail that reinforced my commitment to hosting Family Science Nights: "I was not encouraged to study science/math when I was growing up due to the time period and to my gender. I am so happy that my daughter will have a different experience [growing up]."

Sandra generously shared these feelings after volunteering and participating at a Family Science Night I coordinated at the school our daughters attend. The desire Sandra has to expose her young daughter to science is a position that was echoed in the article in the *Hechinger Report*, where the findings of a study in the March 2010 *International Journal of Science Education* were reported earlier in this section (p. xiv).

While writing this book, I asked my second-grade daughter her thoughts about Family Science Nights and whether she could think of any good things about the two she had already experienced. She responded: "Some people don't really understand science, so when you go to Science Night, you learn a lot about science, but at the same time you are having a lot of fun." I then asked if having her dad and me join her for Science Night was a good thing. To that she said: "Yeah. You get to spend quality time with your parents, and most kids like to have fun with their families."

My daughter was right. A Family Science Night should be viewed as fun-filled quality time where everyone, including parents, can learn a lot.

Who Will Benefit from This Family Science Night Book?

Any organizer from public and private organizations who is aiming to plan a quality, volunteer-run Family Science Night for students in kindergarten through fifth grade will benefit from this book. This includes the following people:

- teachers
- administrators
- directors of curriculum and instruction
- secretaries of education
- leaders of community organizations, including the Parent Teacher Association (PTA), community centers, libraries, after-school programs, and athletic teams
- directors of museums and science centers

How Will Organizers Benefit from This Book?

Family Science Night organizers will benefit from the wealth of step-by-step guidelines, suggestions, and reproducible materials that are included in this book. The contents are conveniently organized into two parts: Part I: Getting Started and Part II: Action Toolkit.

The Getting Started section highlights the actions organizers need to take to plan an effective Family Science Night. Whether you are working with a large or a small planning committee, planning for a small or large event, or targeting one or more grade levels, this guide will direct your attention to the important aspects of any Family Science Night. It specifically focuses on the following:

- finding funding (Chapter 1)
- setting up a planning committee (Chapter 2)
- getting volunteers (Chapter 3)
- buying and storing materials (Chapter 4)
- setting up stations (Chapter 5)

The Action Toolkit features 22 stations you can set up for your Family Science Night. It specifically includes reproducible 8½ × 11 Family Fun Cards organizers can photocopy and set up at each station to give families a set of easy-to-follow instructions. The cards also identify the eight stations that feature make-and-take crafts and show families how they can "Experience More at Home."

In addition to the 22 Family Fun Cards, the Action Toolkit includes a checklist organizers can use to set up each station. Each checklist highlights the supplies organizers will need, retail Web sites and stores that may carry them, a simple illustration of the activity, and a page that details how the station should be set up.

Wrapping It Up

A Family Science Night is just one way to inch the nation forward in its quest to promote children's natural curiosity and to be a leader in science in the world. The two parts of this book (Getting Started and the Action Toolkit) will direct you to the materials you will need to engage families in fun, meaningful, hands-on science that aligns with standards. This book will equip you with the reproducible instruction cards and checklists that will help you set up your stations safely and effectively.

PART I

Getting Started

ONE

Finding Funding

Family Science Nights are an incredible way to connect families with the kinds of hands-on activities that lead to critical thinking, standards-based content, and good old-fashioned fun. This first chapter of Getting Started identifies creative ways to find funding for your Family Science Night at your public or private organization.

Finding Funding

Money, money, money! A Family Science Night requires money—whether large or small, a first-run event, or the tenth annual. The typical costs include purchasing materials for stations and photocopying or laminating materials.

Brainstorm local organizations that may take interest in providing science enrichment for families; then research their charitable-giving criteria to determine whether your Science Night and the organization you represent qualifies for funding. You may be pleasantly surprised with the opportunities you uncover.

Colleges and science-based companies are often very eager to sponsor or participate in Family Science Nights. Pennsylvania State University (Penn State), for example, is one of several colleges and universities that host a Family Science Night at least once or twice a year. As highlighted on the university's Eberly College of Science Web site:

> The cost of funding a single Family Science Night is generally covered through multiple small grants and in-kind donations from the schools. The Outreach Office has partnered with local businesses, which provide monetary donations as well as door prizes, in order to defray the cost of the event. (Eberly College of Science)

Here are some other businesses or organizations you can contact for funding.

- small businesses
- large chain retailers
- your local Parent Teacher Association (PTA) or Parent Teacher Organization (PTO)
- colleges and universities in your town
- your local library

A Vignette

I strongly recommend developing a partnership with the Parent Teacher Association (PTA) or Parent Teacher Organization (PTO) if your school has one. My experience partnering with the PTA at my daughters' school has been stellar; Science Nights would not have been as impactful as they have been without the generous funding it gives. The PTA typically donates hundreds of dollars toward the cost of materials or to rent stations that complement the stations I set up. The past couple of years, for example, the PTA rented a portable planetarium for our families to enjoy! The traveling planetarium, known as the Sky Dome, enabled more than 200 students and their families to experience the wonder of constellations and other aspects of astronomy. Survey data I collected at the end of the night indicated that the Sky Dome was one of the favorite stations among our participants. Consider setting up a mobile planetarium for your Family Science Night and using the Fun Card in the Action Toolkit with it.

What the Research Says about Funding Family Science Nights

Here are a few practical examples:

- The Johnson County Library in Overland Park, Kansas, creatively used a $500 budget to attract hundreds of participants as it partnered with KC Science, Inc. for a highly anticipated Family Science Night. As reported on the Web page for the Urban Libraries Council, the library was the venue for Science Nights through grant funding for three years and was determined to continue having the Science Nights when funding dissipated.

  The library creatively, and perhaps unorthodoxly, fused its summer reading program budget into funding for a Family Science Night that would kick off the summer reading program. The premise was to transform the library into a science museum of sorts by inviting exhibitors to offer as many hands-on station activities as possible, while showcasing its own science-based library books at the same time. The summer reading budget of $500, as described by the Urban Libraries Council, was 100% devoted to purchasing door prizes from evaluation forms-turned-door-prize entries. Door prizes included science toys and mp3 players with preloaded audiobooks. Exhibitors included science fair winners, science club members, and representatives from area universities and science organizations, such as the Kansas City Zoo, NASA, and the local environmental department. The free overhead of the library venue, the science activities provided by the exhibitors, and the $500 summer reading budget devoted to door prizes created an economically stable Family Science Night that is expected to continue for years to come.

- Sandia National Laboratories in New Mexico provides Family Science Nights for elementary students and their families free of charge, and as reported on its Web site, the cost of the event is absorbed by the Lockheed Martin company (www.sandia.gov).
- A mini publication titled "Organizing a Family Science Night at Your School" from author Lloyd H. Barrow suggests creating an RSVP form with a tear-off section that lists the materials needed for stations. The goal is for families to check off any materials they can donate and return the form to the school. Barrow suggests sending the form home at least four to five weeks before the event so there will be time to find other sources to provide materials if needed.
- A first-run Science Night that was the result of a unique partnership between the New York Islanders professional hockey team and the Long Island Science Center charged a $29 admission for each guest and was held at the Nassau Veterans Memorial Coliseum. As reported by D. Hochman on the Islanders' Web site, tickets to the memorable event were limited. This was good because it limited the number of people who could attend and the number of materials that needed to be purchased.

Wrapping It Up

Finding funding for your Family Science Night can be easier than you think. You can start by brainstorming the community and corporate relationships you have and following those leads to help you get the materials you need to run a successful event. Get creative and be motivated—where there's a will (to find funding) there's a way (to find funding).

TWO

Forming a Planning Committee

Establishing a planning committee that can work well together and that is passionate about Family Science Nights is a recipe for success. Your committee should include at least one person who has the power to make decisions at your site or can meet with someone who does. It's a good idea for your committee to include a teacher, a parent, and a PTA member (if applicable) to get balanced input.

A Vignette

Every summer, I meet with parents, PTA members, principals, the assistant superintendent, and the director of science curriculum from a local district to discuss Family Science Nights for the upcoming year. I also meet with parents and PTA members. These individuals form my planning committee for that district. Together we discuss dates for the events, building spaces we could use, and ways to engage teacher, student, and parent volunteers, and we brainstorm challenges we may need to overcome.

Planning Committee Considerations

As you sit down to meet with your planning committee, consider these four questions to get your planning conversation going:

1. What is the best way to recruit teachers to participate?
2. Do you want student volunteers to host stations or welcome participants? What role should parents and community members play in organizing or hosting a Family Science Night?

3. What safety items do we need?
4. Which grade levels will be invited? Is there a particular theme you would like to center the night around?

These four questions should spark healthy conversation that will get the creative juices between you and your planning committee flowing.

1. *What is the best way to recruit teachers to participate?*

   Your planning committee, if it includes representatives from your school or organization, should know the most effective route for encouraging teacher participation.

A Vignette

I sat down with the principal at my daughter's school when I first started organizing Family Science Nights there and found that the best way to recruit teachers for that school was to simply draft a form that pinpointed the information I needed from each teacher. The principal then tweaked the wording as needed and forwarded the form to her teachers. She orally encouraged the teachers to participate as well by talking about Family Science Nights at staff meetings. This was a very simple and painless process for me to follow, and it yielded a great deal of teacher participation. I could not have been happier.

One important point to remember, however, is that I had already formed a positive working relationship with the principal, the teachers, and the students, which presented an obvious advantage. When planning Family Science Nights with other schools with which I did not have such a personal connection, I relied on the representative who had invited me to work to determine the best way to recruit teachers to participate.

2. *Do you want student volunteers to host stations or welcome participants? What role should parents and community members play in organizing or hosting a Family Science Night?*

   How cool would it be for students to see their older brothers or sisters, neighbors, cousins, church members, or friends hosting stations? Such hosts could be upper classmates at the school or alumni, or use some other creative twist on connecting student volunteers to the event. Chances are the student volunteers will be so excited about participating in the event that they will naturally and automatically become a type of public relations committee, spreading the word about the station(s) they will be "working" at the upcoming Family Science Night. It is a wonderful way to engage the school community. If your planning committee supports it, go for it!

Engaging parents in hosting stations or planning for Family Science Night is another phenomenal way to engage the school community and spur enthusiasm for the event among the families there. As with teacher and student recruits, work with your planning committee members to make time to determine the proper protocol to follow in soliciting participation, as long as they are open to the idea. If they are, you are well on your way to synthesizing a healthy amount of engagement by your school community or organization!

3. *What safety items do we need?*

   It is important to remember to talk to your planning committee about safety matters and whether they are your responsibility or the responsibility of personnel at the site. In your conversation with the planning committee or representatives from the site you are using, aim to ask the following six questions:

   - Are fire permits required when hosting events? Who should file for them?
   - What is the maximum occupancy of the facility?
   - How should spills be handled during the event?
   - Is there a certain amount of space that should be kept clear in front of each fire exit?
   - Are there food restrictions for the stations? For example, can peanut butter be included at stations if labeled? (NOTE: None of the stations in the Action Toolkit include peanut butter, but you may be interested in crafting a station of your own that does.)

4. *Which grade levels will be invited? Is there a particular theme you would like to center the night around?*

   An article in the January 2011 issue of *Science and Children* magazine described Math and Science Nights where schools focus on only one grade level at a time (Hatton & Sullivan, 2011). This way, all the activities center on a specific group of students each time. For example, the article describes a fourth-grade Math and Science Night in which students and their parents used straws and marshmallows to build a tower strong enough to hold a plate of cookies as part of an engineering theme. A second-grade night focuses on birds. The school kicks off each grade level's night with an opening activity and ends the evening with a challenge activity that digs deeper into the topic. The rationale the authors give for focusing on one grade level at a time is to give families the opportunity to learn about a topic at length, to focus families' attention on specific learning standards in math and science, and to highlight corresponding parts of the school's curriculum that demonstrate those standards.

Wrapping It Up

Choose committee members who are passionate about planning a successful Family Science Night. Including a member(s) who has authority at the site where the event will take place is a definite bonus. Use the questions in this chapter as conversation starters to get the planning under way with your committee!

THREE

Getting Volunteers

The right volunteers can truly yield a successful Family Science Night. The key to finding the right volunteers is to be creative in brainstorming the types of participants you'd like to invite to be part of your event.

Be Creative When Selecting Volunteers

Brainstorm reputable groups of students and adults from your organization and community who may enjoy interacting with K–5 students and their families—representatives from medical practices, fitness facilities, blood banks, scientific laboratories, community colleges, universities, and more. Doing so makes a connection with your local community, which is a notable goal for any Family Science Night. Your list of reputable volunteers could include the following:

- college students
- middle and high school students
- parents
- teachers
- local doctors, nurses, fitness experts, and scientists
- school administrators
- Girl Scouts and Boy Scouts of America

Working with Students

One of the greatest rewards I have had organizing Family Science Nights has been working with the students who host stations. Middle school students to high school seniors are phenomenal in the amount of enthusiasm, knowledge, and professionalism they bring to the evening. With a little bit of training in the hours before the event, students tend to do a fantastic job of engaging the families who visit their stations. Here are some tips to keep in mind when working with students:

- Allow students to choose their own stations weeks or months in advance if possible.
- Ask students to arrive at least an hour before the event to become familiar with their station and to test it.
- Arrange for students to work in pairs with each other or with an adult to increase their comfort with hosting stations.

What has always worked well for me is to allow students to choose the station they would like to host by posting a sign-up sheet with a very short description of each station. In most cases, I contact the adviser of the school-based club with which I want to work (such as a high school Key Club or a middle school science club) or the parent of the child I invite to host a station.

Training Volunteers

Whether working with student or adult volunteers, you will need to train them to host their stations well. The following starter questions should guide you to maximize your partnership with volunteers:

- Are you familiar with Family Science Nights?
- Do you have an age-appropriate activity you would like to share or would you be interested in operating one of our stations?
- What pieces of equipment or pictures would you be interested in sharing with children and their families that would be safe for them to touch or hold (stethoscope, microscope, X-rays, photographs, blood pressure cuff, scale, etc.)?
- What can we do to make your time at our Family Science Night mutually beneficial?

A Vignette

My experience with students and adult volunteers has been remarkable. Parents, students, and teachers alike have had positive words to say about their experiences as a Family Science Night volunteer. Here's what parent volunteers have said about Family Science Nights:

> I just wanted to thank you again for your amazing administration of Science Night. I have always been such a science nerd (it's true!), and it was so satisfying to see these young kids getting so involved in their experiments and excited to learn. So much of the school system nowadays is solely preparation for standardized testing, and the fact that you brought a love for science into the school atmosphere was incredibly reassuring and encouraging. —Adult volunteer

> I was so impressed with the entire Science [Night]. It was so well done. You were a big hit with the teens also. The one young woman could not stop talking about how excited she was to meet you and was so happy that you gave her your contact information. —Student volunteer

> Thanks again for the offer to help—I appreciate how much you've involved me even though I work! —Adult volunteer

If you give your volunteers the right information, your Family Science Night is sure to be mutually beneficial for all. You'll need to give them at least the following level of detail:

- the date, time, and location of the event
- the time they should arrive
- ways to contact you or another representative by phone, by e-mail, or in person
- their roles and responsibilities as volunteers
- the station(s) they will be operating, or another role they will play
- what they should wear
- the procedure they should follow in the event of an emergency at the event (students' accidentally swallowing objects, fire, choking, etc.)

What you want is to give your volunteers the details they need to run their stations with confidence.

A Vignette

The manager of a station at a Family Science Night I hosted shared that one of the operators said the setup directions for her activity were not clear which made her nervous about engaging students at her station.

I was reminded of something that night—it is critical to set aside time to ensure that each volunteer fully understands the instructions for his or her station, no matter how clear you believe the instructions are, and to *listen* to the volunteers' concerns. As a result of that night, I make sure either I or a representative from my team checks in with each volunteer before participants arrive to ensure everything is OK, thank them, and give them a vote of confidence.

Wrapping It Up

You need good volunteers to be able to run a successful Family Science Night. Think about the opportunities you have for volunteers, then be creative with the people you can ask to help. Consider asking both students and adults you can trust from your community. Use the four starter questions from this chapter to get the conversations going with your potential volunteers!

FOUR

Buying and Storing Materials

The key to buying materials for a Family Science Night is to know how much and from where—how much do they cost and from where should they be purchased? The key to storing materials is to know in what and where—what kind of container should you store them in and where should the containers be kept?

A Vignette

The first time I coordinated a Family Science Night, the number of people I could reasonably expect was a complete toss-up. There was no point of reference for the number of participants I should expect. Since it was operated under the auspices of the PTA, the closest estimation I had was the number of people who attended PTA-sponsored family nights with other themes that were offered on the same day of the week at the same site. The amount of materials I should buy was somewhat of a mystery. To get a sense of the number of people planning to attend, I included a detachable RSVP form at the bottom of a flyer I sent to families at the school hosting the event.

The first year there were approximately 150 RSVP responses—children and adults included. That night, approximately 175 participants attended. Each year thereafter, attendance continued to grow and grow. As the number of participants grew, so did the amount of materials I bought (and stored).

As you develop a plan of how many materials to buy and from where, consider these tips:

Tips for Buying Materials for Family Science Nights

- Use the Organizer's Checklists in the Action Toolkit section of this book to see which consumable and reusable materials you will need for each station.
- Research two or three retailers that carry the materials you need and find their current prices, for comparison shopping.
- Use your organization's tax-exempt card to avoid paying tax on materials if you are a qualifying nonprofit entity.
- Talk with store managers or other representatives about your Science Night to determine whether discounts (or donations) are available.

A number of online and retail stores sell materials that are perfectly suited for Family Science Nights and offer reasonable prices. Here are some of my favorite retailers:

- Steve Spangler Science (www.stevespanglerscience.com)
- Science Kit (sciencekit.com)
- Educational Innovations (www.teachersource.com)
- Carolina Biological (www.carolinoa.com)
- Amazon (www.amazon.com)
- Walmart (www.walmart.com)
- Staples (www.staples.com)
- Dollar Tree (www.dollartree.com)
- Target (www.target.com)

These companies feature kits and individually packaged items you may find useful in supporting hands-on investigations. Even more, companies such as Steve Spangler Science feature instructional videos you can watch online and science activities that can be complemented by children's books as well. Science Kit and Educational Innovations, for example, offer materials that are of great quality at affordable prices. Staples offers lab coats, safety glasses, and other scientific tools you may want to include at your stations. Not all station materials have to be purchased as kits. Some may require only household products, which is true of several stations in the Action Toolkit of this book. Three retail stores I have found to be affordable are Walmart, Dollar Tree, and Target.

Storing Materials

After you've purchased your materials, you'll need to think about a place to store them. To store and where to store—that is the question. You can start figuring this out by reading the labels on each product to determine whether there are specific ways they need to be stored for safety reasons. The materials for the Family Science Nights I host are routinely stored in one of two places—a) labeled, plastic bins or b) labeled cardboard boxes—in temperature-controlled environments. Plastic bins are naturally the preferred storage containers since they are waterproof, lidded, and can be see-through. Cardboard can work just as well if all liquids in or around the box(es) are tightly sealed in plastic bags or containers so the box and its contents do not become soiled.

Wrapping It Up

The tips for buying materials that are included in this chapter can guide you on your quest to find the retailer and prices that will work best for your Family Science Night. Keep in mind that the key to buying materials for a Family Science Night is to know how much and from where—how much do they cost and from where should they be purchased? The key to storing materials is to know in what and where—what kind of container should they be stored in and where should the containers be kept? The Organizer's Checklists in the Action Toolkit section of this book will point you in the right direction for buying your materials. Take advantage of your resources!

FIVE

Planning Your Stations

Kids like to have fun. Child development research has shown that certain experiences are highly beneficial for young children, evoking feelings of happiness, comfort, and ultimately fun. In *Foundations for Early Childhood Education* (2007), author Janet Gonzalez-Mena wrote: "a knowledge of child development helps adults predict strategies, materials, interactions, and experiences that will be safe, healthy, interesting, achievable, and challenging to children" (p. 41). According to this type of research, some of the best experiences children can have are when they

- explore, create, and respond to things
- imagine, express their feelings, and use the five senses
- observe, compare, and classify
- acquire facts, make patterns, and recall information
- take pride in their accomplishments

Each activity in the Action Toolkit of this book embodies one or more of those types of experiences.

Characteristics of Effective Stations

At least three characteristics should be included at each station to engage elementary students and their families in hands-on science:

1. simple, easy-to-follow instructions printed in large font
2. open-ended questions that will encourage discussion between parents and children
3. a list of simple at-home activities parents and children can do to continue learning science at their leisure

1. *Display Simple Instructions for Parents and Children to Follow*

   Each Family Science Night station should position parents to easily lead and engage their children in the activity it features. Taking time to ensure parents are properly empowered to engage their children in each activity is crucial because, in essence, they play the role of the "museum guide." If the parents do not know what to do, chances are the children will not either—at least not to the extent the organizer wishes. The children may still be inclined to touch and interact with the station activities but not with the same level of engagement and understanding that would result if parents were properly equipped with station instructions that were simple and easy to follow.

2. *Display Questions to Encourage Discussion Between Parents and Children*

   Getting kids to ask questions is an easy thing to do. It's part of their natural curiosity. As Kimberly Brenneman (2009) of Rutgers University suggests, children naturally look for answers to questions about their surroundings by interacting with it so they can learn more about it. At the "Fishing for Planets" station in the Action Toolkit, for example, parents can ask their child simple yet inquisitive questions like: which planet is the largest? which planet is closest to the sun? how does the planet you caught stick to the fishing pole? For the "Fossil Hunt" station, parents can ask: how many trace fossils did you find? where do you think people can find trace fossils? For the "Animal Tessellations" section, parents can ask: how many tessellations do you see? what other kind of animal would you like to make a tessellation out of?

   The key point to stress to parents would be that the questions they ask do not have to be questions that have a right or wrong answer. They just need to be questions that get kids to open up about what they're thinking about the activity. When questions that do have a right or wrong answer come up, like how do boats float, parents can always keep a list of questions that arise from Family Science Night and research the answer at home, in a library, or through a book or computer that's available at the event.

3. *Provide a List of Simple Activities Parents and Children Can Explore at Home*

   A well-organized and executed Family Science Night is an excellent venue to excite young children about science, further knowledge, and connect their parents to science standards. Yet the fun and learning should not stop there; it should continue at home. Consider giving families a short list of activities they can do at home to extend their Family Science Night activities.

In a 2009 article in *Young Children*, authors Crawford, Heaton, Heslop, and Kixmiller overwhelmingly supported science learning at home, sharing that one of the best effects is when children begin showing interest in starting their own scientific investigations at home. This same feeling is shared by the National Science Teachers Association, which publicly iterates the important role parents play on a daily basis to help children learn scientific concepts and skills, just by letting them play and investigate with supervision at home.

Wrapping It Up

Family Science Night has to be loads and loads of fun—otherwise it's pointless! There are certain experiences child development research has shown to be highly beneficial for young children because they evoke feelings of happiness and a high level of comfort. The focal point of this chapter was to highlight those experiences and three ways they can shine through the stations you plan. Make the stations you plan for your Family Science Night a whole lot of fun!

PART II

The Action Toolkit

The Action Toolkit

This Action Toolkit equips you with 22 stations you can include in your Family Science Night! For each station you will find at least four valuable pages of easy-to-use resources:

- Family Fun Card
- The Organizer's Checklist

How the Family Fun Cards Engage Families

- The Family Fun Cards are a great way to engage your families in the fun learning opportunities at each station! Photocopy each set of cards, laminate them or put them in sheet protectors, and stand them up in plain sight on book stands or file folders for families to see.
- Families will be able to engage in each station through these four, easy-to-follow sections:
    1. Explore
    2. Expected Result
    3. Explanation
    4. Experience More at Home
- To enrich families' at-home experience and the probability that they will continue the fun science learning at home, photocopy the Experience More at Home section of each Family Fun Card, and compile a booklet of the Family Fun Cards for families to take with them. This way, families can engage in the stations through hands-on activities and dialogue and do follow-up activities at home.

How Can the Family Fun Cards Help the Station Hosts?

- The station hosts should follow the instructions in the Explore section of the Family Fun Card for their station to help them test the activity before participants arrive.
- Each host should also take a minute to read over the Expected Result and Explanation sections of the Family Fun Card to be familiar with the kind of explanation to give families if asked.
- Hosts should be familiar with the handling, storage, disposal, ingestion, inhalation, and skin contact sections of the material safety data sheets (MSDS) listed in the Safety category of the Organizer's Checklists when applicable.
- Hosts should also become familiar with the learning objectives for their stations so they will have a good idea of what participants should learn as their take-away messages.

Index and Learning Objectives for Family Science Night Stations

Family Science Night Station	**Learning Objectives Students will ...**
Animal Tessellations	▪ Understand that a tessellation is a repeating pattern ▪ Make a repeating pattern with animal shapes to create a tessellation
Baby Bottle ... Pop!	▪ Understand the definition of gas pressure ▪ Compare the pressure of bottles with varying amounts of gas pressure
Bloody Fingers	▪ Observe what happens when acids and bases mix ▪ Discover how litmus paper changes color to show whether something is an acid or a base
Bubble Glove	▪ Understand that certain ingredients can make strong bubbles ▪ Experiment with bouncing bubbles on a glove ▪ Use a scientific tool to create a bubble wand
Bubble Shapes	▪ Create geometric shapes using plastic sticks ▪ Discover that plastic geometric shapes can create geometric bubble shapes
Clay Boat	▪ Build a clay boat and test how well it floats ▪ Understand that capacity shows how much someone or something can hold ▪ Discover the capacity of their clay boat

(continued)

Family Science Night Station	**Learning Objectives Students will ...**
Cover Your Bases	▪ Use scientific tools to test whether a liquid is an acid or a base ▪ Discover what happens when acids and bases mix
Crazy Worm	▪ Understand that polymers act like liquids and solids at the same time ▪ Experiment with a polymer they create
Fingerprint ID	▪ Understand that all fingerprints are unique ▪ Discover how to make a type 14 flat impression fingerprint ▪ Use scientific tools to examine different types of fingerprints ▪ Identify the pattern of their fingerprint
Fishing for Planets	▪ Become familiar with the eight planets in Earth's solar system ▪ Use fine motor skills to fish for planets with magnetic fishing poles
Floating Balls	▪ Understand that Bernoulli's principle shows how airplanes can fly ▪ Demonstrate Bernoulli's principle by balancing plastic balls in a stream of air
Fossil Hunt	▪ Become familiar with the tools scientists use to search for fossils ▪ Identify and sort two types of fossils: trace and body
Germ Glow	▪ Recognize that hands carry germs ▪ Discover where germs can hide on dry hands ▪ Become familiar with good hand-washing techniques
Marker Magic	▪ Understand that rubbing alcohol is a chemical that can make permanent marker "bleed," or spread ▪ Use scientific tools to demonstrate how rubbing alcohol and permanent marker can create tie-dye squares
Mobile Planetarium	▪ Become familiar with planets and stars from our solar system ▪ Create and name a unique constellation and write a short story that tells how it got its name
Move to the Beat	▪ Distinguish between a resting heart rate and an active heart rate ▪ Use technology to discover and compare resting and active heart rates
Paint a Mold	▪ Use scientific tools to study animal tracks and match them to the animals that made them ▪ Create an animal track of their own (optional)

(continued)

Family Science Night Station	Learning Objectives Students will ...
Paper Airplane	▪ Design a paper airplane ▪ Discover that different airplanes fly at different speeds ▪ Calculate the speed and/or distance of their own airplanes
Soapy Boat	▪ Understand that soap can be used to power foil boats ▪ Experiment with different dish soaps to see which makes a boat move more quickly
Super Bubble	▪ Understand that certain ingredients make large, stretchy bubbles ▪ Compare and experiment with two different bubble recipes to determine which makes the larger bubbles
Super Sand	▪ Understand that certain chemicals make objects hydrophobic, or repelled by ("afraid" of) water ▪ Experiment with hydrophobic objects
Wacky Ball	▪ Understand the definition of density ▪ Compare the densities of objects that are the same size

Animal Tessellations

Family Fun Card

What pattern can you make with animal shapes?

Explore:

1. A tessellation is a pattern made of shapes. Each shape is drawn over and over again in a way that the shapes fit together like a puzzle.
2. Choose an animal template to draw on your paper.
3. Trace your template one time on your paper.
4. Solve the mystery of which animal parts fit together by turning your template so it fits with your tracing like a puzzle. You may have to try moving your template to different parts of your tracing until you get a good fit.
5. Keep repeating your pattern until the paper is filled. Make sure you do not have any spaces or gaps between your tracings.
6. Color in the pattern to add the finishing touches!

Fun Fact: Soccer balls, basketball nets, chessboards, and turtle shells are examples of tessellations.

Animal Tessellations

Family Fun Card

Expected Result:

You should be able to make a pattern using the animal-shape template. Turn the template so that it fits the pattern like a puzzle each time you trace it. There should be no gaps or overlaps.

Explanation:

Tessellations are patterns that are made with one or more shapes. You can use geometric shapes (squares, triangles, rectangles), animal shapes, or other shapes. The shape is turned to fit like a puzzle each time it is drawn. There should be no gaps and no overlaps each time the shape is drawn.

Experience More at Home:

Go to www.tessellations.org to see tessellations from kids and to learn to make tessellations with two or more shapes.

The Organizer's Checklist for

Animal Tessellations

Station Checklist			
Materials:	Reusable		Sample tessellations
			Tessellation templates
	Consumable		White paper
			Crayons
			Pencils
Retailers:	Tessellation templates can be purchased online from eNasco (www.enasco.com) or Amazon (www.amazon.com). All other materials can be purchased from small businesses or large chain retailers.		

Setup Instructions for

Animal Tessellations

Tessellation Templates

1. Prepare a sample animal tessellation to display, or find one in a book or an online resource.
2. Gather the templates, crayons, white paper, and pencils.

Tips on the Animal Tessellations

This station is very easy to set up and requires very few materials, yet it engages participants in deep thinking. What is most important to convey as you help participants tessellate their animal shapes is different parts of the animal shape can fit together like a puzzle. Their task is to solve the mystery of which parts of the animal fit like a lock-and-key. Having samples of the tessellations and numbering each shape after it's drawn will really help convey this central message.

Display

Spread out the sample tessellations you prepared (or gathered from other resources), animal tessellation templates, white paper, pencils, and crayons for participants to use. If servicing a large crowd, consider setting out a hundred or so sheets of paper at a time and replenishing the supply as needed so participants are less inclined to use numerous sheets at once. Set out the Family Fun Card in plain view for participants to use.

Baby Bottle ... Pop!

Family Fun Card

Which bottle has more pressure trapped inside?

Explore:

1. Put on safety glasses to protect your eyes.
2. Squeeze the baby bottle with the antacid and the bottle with water.
3. Compare how easy or hard it is to squeeze the bottles.

Now you try to create gas pressure!

4. Draw a picture of the empty baby bottle with the nipple on top.
5. Put one antacid tablet in a baby bottle filled with 8 ounces of water.
6. Screw the nipple on right away, and watch it for a few seconds.
7. Draw a picture of what happened to the nipple.
8. Did you create gas pressure? How do you know?

Baby Bottle ... Pop!

Family Fun Card

Expected Result:

You should see the nipple on the baby bottle get bigger and bigger as the antacid dissolves in the water.

You should also be able to feel the difference between the baby bottle that has water and the bottle that has water and the antacid. The bottle with the antacid should be hard to squeeze, and the bottle with the water should be easy.

Explanation:

The antacids make a gas when they dissolve in water. As the gas from the antacid fills the baby bottle, the "blind" nipple (which does not have a hole in it) gets larger while the bottle becomes harder and harder to squeeze.

The nipple gets larger and the bottle becomes harder to squeeze because of the force the gas puts on it. The force of gas on an object is called gas pressure.

This baby bottle activity cannot be used to measure the amount of gas an antacid makes because the nipple gets stretched out each time it is used, so the measurements will be different each time.

Experience More at Home:

Use a balloon and bottle to discover foods that produce gas, such as soft drinks and yeast.

The Organizer's Checklist for Baby Bottle … Pop!

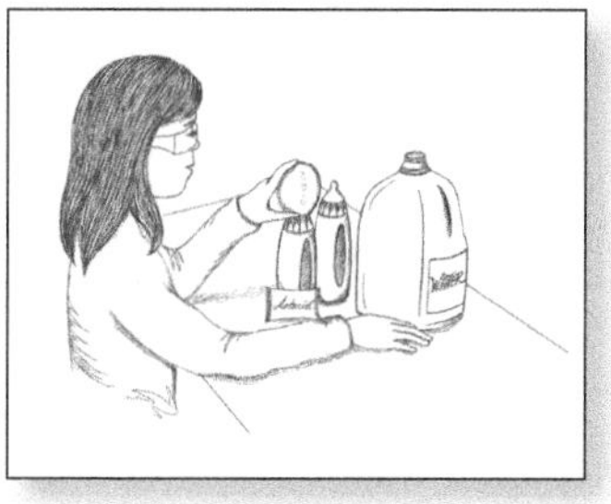

Station Checklist			
Materials:	Reusable		Safety glasses
			Baby bottles
			"Blind" baby bottle nipples (without a hole)
			Plastic container with a lid (to hold the antacid tablets)
			Large empty container (to discard water)
			Books about gas pressure (optional)
	Consumable		Water
			Masking tape
			Antacid tablets (e.g., Alka-Seltzer)
			Crayons
			White drawing paper
	Safety		MSDS for the antacid you chose
Retailers:	Safety glasses can be ordered from Staples (www.staples.com), Lakeshore Learning Store (www.lakeshorelearning.com), and Amazon (www.amazon.com). Other retailers can be found through an Internet search with keywords "safety glasses for kids." "Blind" baby bottles can be purchased from Steve Spangler Science (www.stevespangler.com) or from small businesses. Material safety data sheets (MSDS) can be found online by doing an Internet search using the keywords "MSDS" and the name of the antacid you chose. For example, "MSDS for Alka-Seltzer." All other materials can be purchased from other online retailers, small businesses, or large chain retailers.		

Setup Instructions for

Baby Bottle ... Pop!

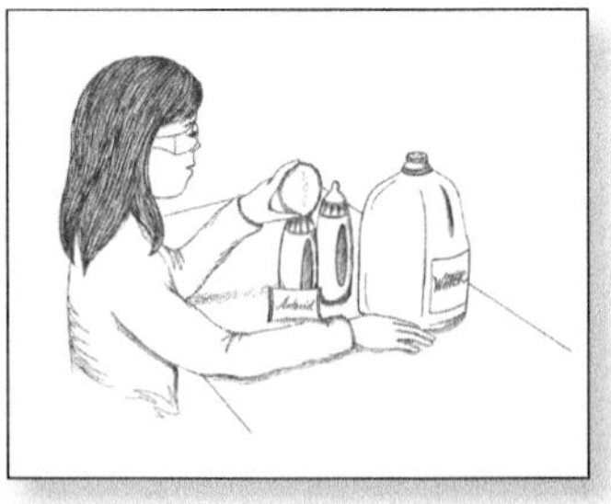

The Baby Bottles

1. Label one bottle "Water Only" and the other "Water and Antacid."
2. Fill the Water Only bottle with water. Screw on the nipple and top. Add masking tape around the top to discourage participants from opening it. Have enough water on hand for each participant to pour about 8 ounces of water into the Water and Antacid bottle.
3. Fill the Water and Antacid bottle with water. Loosely screw on the nipple so participants will be able to open it.
4. Have a large empty container for participants to dump their bottles of water or set up the station near a sink.
5. Have a station host to ensure that young participants engage in the activity with a parent and do not eat the antacids (in which case you would refer to the MSDS sheet or the safety instructions on the antacid bottle, or call 911).
6. **Optional:** Set up bottles with different amounts of antacids for participants to feel varying amounts of gas pressure.

Antacids

Provide enough antacids for each participant to use at least two.

Display

Set out the safety glasses, the labeled Water Only bottle, the labeled Water and Antacid bottle, antacids, bottles of water (or have access to a sink), a baby bottle filled with gas pressure and one without, books about gas pressure (optional), and the Family Fun Card on the table.

Bloody Fingers

Family Fun Card

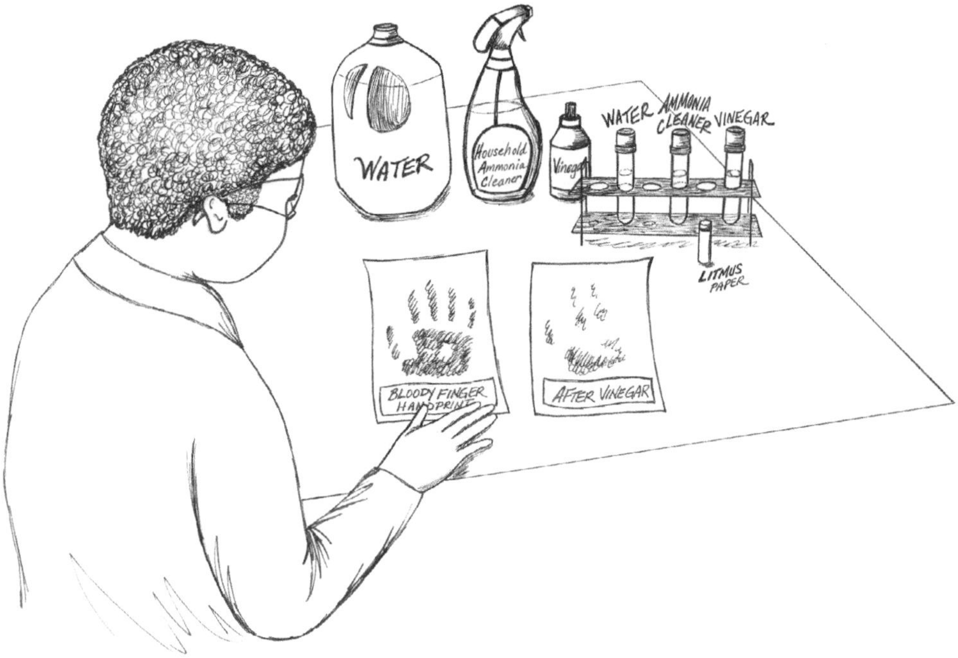

What happens when you mix a "bloody" acid with a base?

Explore:

1. Put on safety glasses.
2. Spray your hand with Bloody Goo and press it on the Magic Paper (or, put on a glove and spray that instead). Do you see "bloody fingers" on the paper (a handprint that turns red)?
3. Use the Disappearing Water to spray the "bloody fingers" you created on the paper. What happens to the fingers now?
4. Discover more about Bloody Goo and Disappearing Water by putting one drop of each liquid on the litmus paper you see.
5. What color did the litmus become? Use the litmus paper color chart to see which liquid is an acid and which is a base.

Bloody Fingers

Family Fun Card

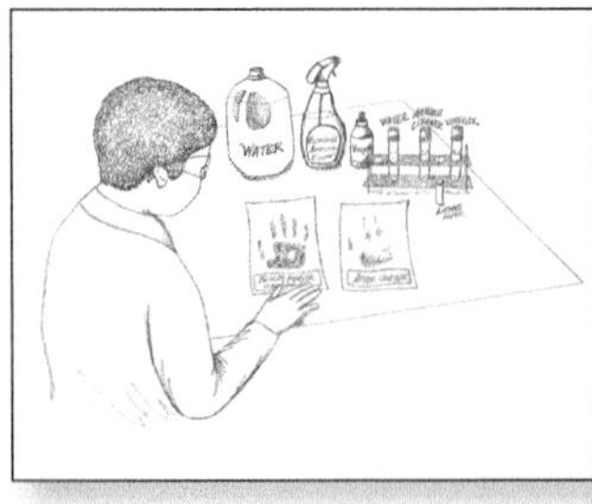

Expected Result:

You should see a red handprint appear on the Magic Paper after you spray your hand with Bloody Goo and press it on the paper. The red print should disappear after the Disappearing Water is sprayed on it. You should be able to use the litmus paper to discover which liquid is an acid and which is a base.

Explanation:

Bloody Goo is a base. Disappearing Water is an acid. Magic Paper (called goldenrod paper for its yellow color) turns red when a base touches it. It turns yellow again when an acid touches it. A base (like Bloody Goo made with ammonia, baking soda or washing solution, and water) loses its oxygen and hydrogen molecules in water. An acid (like Disappearing Water made with lemon juice or vinegar and water) loses its hydrogen molecules when it's in water. When acids and bases mix, they make water and balance each other out. When the Bloody Goo and Disappearing Water mix together they balance each other out, which makes the handprint disappear!

Experience More at Home:

Visit www.kidsknowit.com/interactive-educational-movies/free-online-movies.php?movie=Acids%20And%20Bases to watch a short movie for kids about acids and bases.

The Organizer's Checklist for

Bloody Fingers

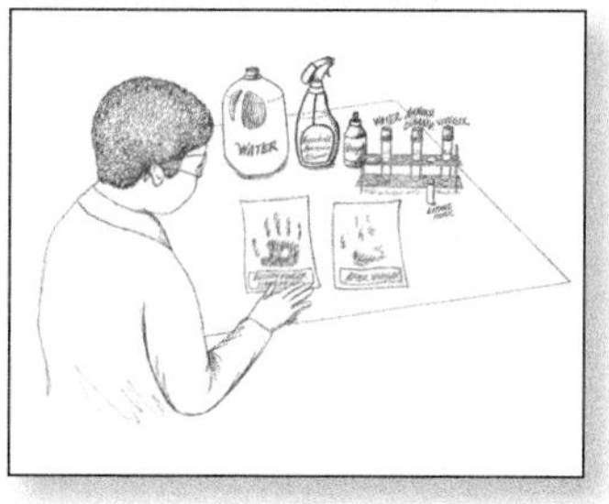

Station Checklist			
Materials:	Reusable		Droppers (or pipettes)
			Safety glasses
			Lab coat (optional)
			Plastic spray bottles (at least two)
			Plastic jars
			Test tubes and test tube racks
	Consumable		Disposable, latex-free gloves (optional)
			Ammonia-based cleaner (such as Windex), baking soda solution, or washing soda
			Water
			Plastic, disposable pipettes
			Goldenrod (Magic) paper, that is chemically treated to be color-changing
			Lemon juice or vinegar (to make Bloody Goo)
			Paper towels
			Litmus paper (to test acids and bases)
	Safety		MSDS for washing soda
			MSDS for ammonia

(continued)

Retailers:	Safety glasses can be ordered from Staples (www.staples.com), Lakeshore Learning Store (www.lakeshorelearning.com), Amazon (www.amazon.com), or other retailers and small businesses. Litmus paper can be purchased from Steve Spangler Science (www.stevespanglerscience.com), Edmund Scientifics (www.scientificsonline.com), Amazon (www.amazon.com), or other retailers and small businesses. Color-changing goldenrod paper can be purchased from Educational Innovations (www.teachersource.com), Steve Spangler Science (www.stevespanglerscience.com), or Amazon (www.amazon.com). Washing soda can be purchased at supermarkets or large chain retailers. It is usually shelved near laundry detergents. Material safety data sheets (MSDS) can be found online using the keywords "MSDS for washing soda" and "MSDS for ammonia."

Setup Instructions for
Bloody Fingers

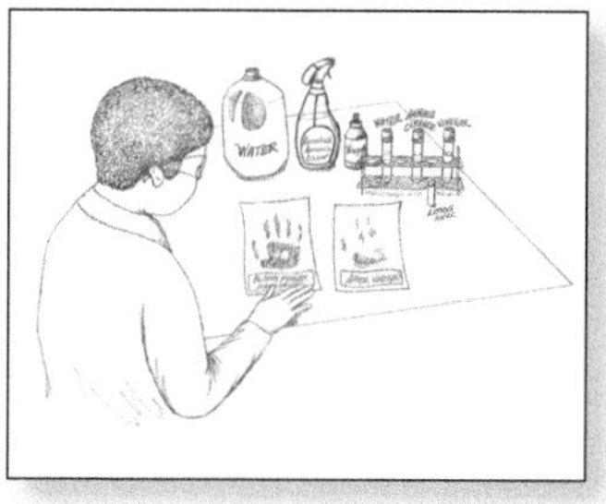

Bloody Goo

1. Label a spray bottle "Bloody Goo."
2. Fill the bottle halfway with household ammonia cleaner and the rest of the way with water. Or you can fill half the bottle with baking soda solution (stir one spoonful of baking soda into 1 quart of water until no more will dissolve) and water.

Disappearing Water

1. Label a spray bottle "Disappearing Water."
2. Fill the bottle halfway with lemon juice and the rest of the way with water (or you can fill it halfway with vinegar and the rest of the way with water).

Determining Acids and Bases

1. Label one test tube "Bloody Goo" and another "Disappearing Water," and set the test tubes in a rack.
2. Have plastic, disposable pipettes (or medicine droppers) available for participants to squeeze a small amount of each solution onto the litmus paper to discover whether it is an acid or a base.

Display

Set out the safety glasses and Family Fun Card in plain view for participants to see and use. Have half sheets of the goldenrod paper with the disposable gloves, Bloody Goo and Disappearing Water bottles, litmus paper, and pipettes (droppers) on the table for participants to use. Also set out a sample "bloody handprint" for participants to see. Just remember to refresh the handprint every now and again since it will disappear after several minutes!

Bubble Glove

Family Fun Card

How many bubbles can you bounce on your hand?

Explore:

1. Cut the fat, rounded end of a disposable pipette to use as a bubble wand, or use a regular bubble wand with a circular end.
2. Put on a clean, cotton glove.
3. Dip the cutoff end of the pipette into a cup of bubble solution.
4. Blow through the small end of the pipette to make a bubble that's any size you want.
5. Gently shake or blow the bubble off the pipette onto the glove.
6. How many times can you bounce the bubble before it pops? Tell a friend next to you.

Bubble Glove

Family Fun Card

Expected Result:

You should be able to gently shake one or more bubbles off the pipette and bounce them on the cotton glove.

Explanation:

Soap and glycerin make bubbles very strong, which makes them able to withstand the gentle pressure of bouncing on a glove. The clean, soft texture of the gloves keeps it from popping the bubbles right away.

Experience More at Home:

Experiment with different bubble recipes to discover which makes the best bubbles.

Discover other materials bubbles can land on without popping.

The Organizer's Checklist for **Bubble Glove**

Station Checklist			
Materials:	Reusable		Cotton gloves
			Scissors
			Plastic cups (to hold pipettes)
			Permanent markers (e.g., Sharpies)
	Consumable		Distilled water
			Glycerin
			Dish soap (Dawn and Joy work well), Extreme Bubble Solution
			2-ounce plastic containers with lids
			Plastic, disposable pipettes
			Disposable gloves (optional)
			Hand sanitizer
	Safety		MSDS for Dawn or Joy, Extreme Bubble Solution, and glycerin
Retailers:	Extreme Bubble Solution can be purchased from Steve Spangler Science (www.stevespanglerscience.com). Glycerin can be purchased from your local pharmacy or large chain retailer. Plastic, disposable pipettes can be purchased from Steve Spangler Science (www.stevespanglerscience.com), Science Bob (www.sciencebob.com), and Amazon (www.amazon.com). They can also be found online by doing an Internet search with keywords "plastic pipette Cartesian." Material safety data sheets (MSDS) can be found by doing an Internet search using the keywords "MSDS for Extreme Bubble Solution," "MSDS for glycerin," and "MSDS" and the name of the dish soap you chose. For example, "MSDS for Dawn." All other materials can be purchased online or from small businesses or large chain retailers.		

Setup Instructions for
Bubble Glove

Bubble Solution

1. At least 24 hours BEFORE the event, prepare bubble solution (5½ cups distilled water, 2 tablespoons glycerin, 3 tablespoons dish soap) OR prepare Extreme Bubble Solution by package directions.
2. Pour about ⅛ cup of bubble solution into lidded 2-ounce containers for participants to keep.
3. Get permanent markers to write their names on their cups of bubble solution.

Cotton Gloves

1. Have clean cotton gloves free of debris for participants to use.
2. Set out hand sanitizer to use before and after putting on the gloves.

Bubble Wand

1. Cut the "fat" ends of the disposable pipettes to use as bubble wands. Use disposable gloves, or wash your hands with soap and water, before handling the pipettes.
2. If using disposable pipettes, each participant should have his or her own.

Display

Set out the cotton gloves, bubble solution (pre-poured), permanent markers, pipettes standing up in cups with narrow ends pointing down (to protect the ends participants will put in their mouths), and the Family Fun Card.

Bubble Shapes

Family Fun Card

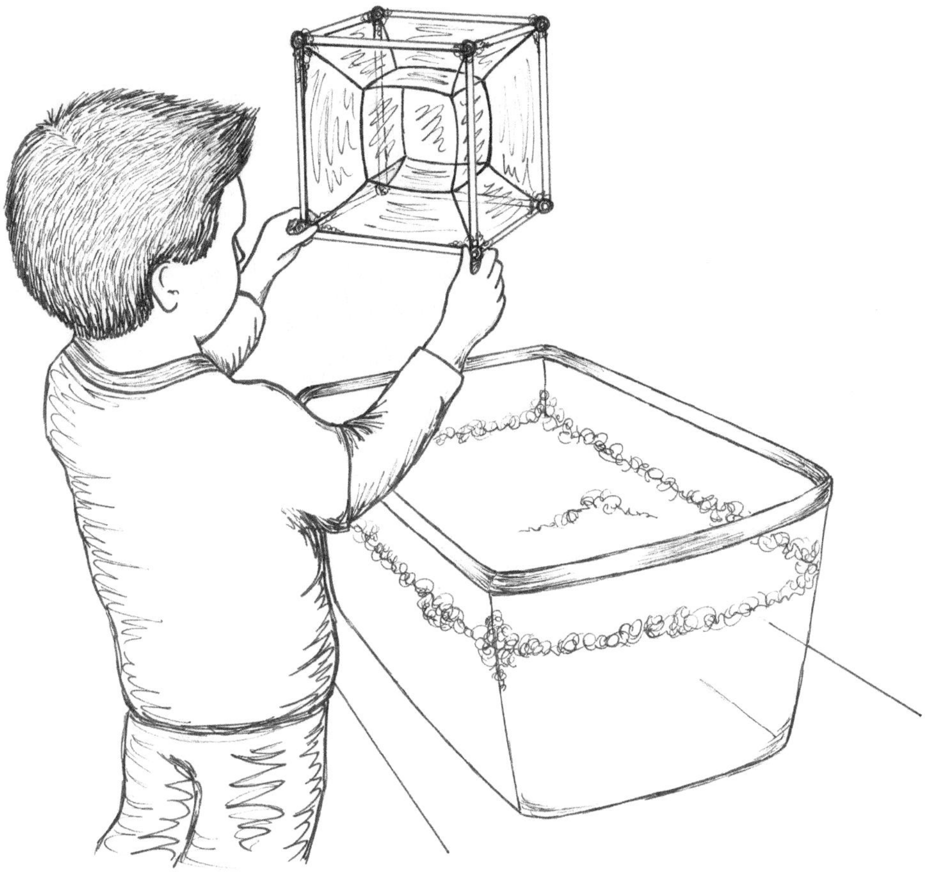

Which bubble shape can you make?

Explore:

1. Use the sticks and connectors to make a shape for your bubble. Be creative!
2. Dip your shape into the tub of bubble solution.
3. Carefully lift the shape out of the bubble tub.
4. What shape is your bubble?
5. Dip your bubble in the bubble solution and watch what happens. Did the shape change?

Bubble Shapes

Family Fun Card

Expected Result:

The bubbles should form in the shape you made with your connectors. If you dipped the shape twice, you should have a bubble in a bubble.

Explanation:

Soap weakens the surface tension, or skin, of water by making it slippery and stretchy. This characteristic makes it easy for the bubbles to stretch into the shapes you make with the sticks and connectors.

Experience More at Home:

www.stevespanglerscience.com/product/square-bubble-maker has a fun video about making square bubbles.

The Organizer's Checklist for
Bubble Shapes

Station Checklist			
Materials:	Reusable		Zome Bubble kit
			Measuring cup
			1-gallon mixing bowl
			3-gallon plastic bin
	Consumable		Distilled water
			Glycerin
			Dish soap (Dawn and Joy work well and fragrance-free is best) OR Extreme Bubble Solution
			Paper towels
	Safety		MSDS for Extreme Bubble Solution
			MSDS for Dawn or Joy
			MSDS for glycerin
Retailers:	Zome Bubble kits can be purchased from Zome Tool (www.zometool.com), Amazon (www.amazon.com), and Fat Brain Toys (www.fatbraintoys.com). Extreme Bubble Solution can be purchased from Steve Spangler Science (www.stevespanglerscience.com). Glycerin can be purchased from your local pharmacy or large chain retailer. Material safety data sheets (MSDS) can be found by doing an Internet search using the keywords "MSDS for Extreme Bubble Solution," "MSDS for glycerin," and "MSDS" and the name of the dish soap you chose. For example, "MSDS for Dawn." All other materials can be purchased online or from small businesses or large chain retailers.		

Setup Instructions for **Bubble Shapes**

Bubble Solution

1. At least 24 hours BEFORE the event, prepare bubble solution (5½ cups distilled water, 25 mL glycerin, 40 mL dish soap)

   OR

   Purchase and prepare Extreme Bubble Solution according to package directions.
2. Pour several gallons of the bubble solution you prepared into the large plastic bin. The goal is to pour enough solution to cover the Zome Bubble connector sticks when they are assembled into a shape. Different kits include connectors of different sizes.

Bubble Shapes

Have one or more sets of Zome Bubble connector sticks available for participants to make their bubble shapes.

Display

Set out the large bin of bubble solution, Zome Bubble sticks and connectors, Family Fun Card, and paper towels for participants to use.

Clay Boat

Family Fun Card

What's the capacity of your clay boat?

Explore:

1. Decide on the size and shape you would like your boat to be and make it.
2. Gently place your boat in the water.
3. If it floats, gently place one object in it at a time.
4. The number of objects your boat holds is called its capacity. What's the capacity of your boat?
5. If your boat does not float, try a new design and keep going until it works. You can do it!

Clay Boat

Family Fun Card

Expected Result:

You should be able to build a clay boat and test how well it floats. Then you should be able to count the number of objects it can hold to find its capacity.

Explanation:

To float, a boat has to be a size and shape that will push an amount of water out of the way that's equal to its weight. For example, if the clay boat weighs 1 pound, it has to be able to push 1 pound of water out of the way to float.

The wider the bottom of your boat, the better it should be able to push water out of the way, float, and have more capacity.

Experience More at Home:

Go to www.squidoo.com/why-do-things-float to watch a video to learn more about how things float.

The Organizer's Checklist for

Clay Boat

Station Checklist			
Materials:	Reusable		Clear plastic containers or bowls in which to float the boats
			Weights (pennies, paper clips, binder rings, etc.)
			Plastic containers or cups to hold weights
			Books about capacity, buoyancy, boats, or similar topics (optional)
	Consumable		Water
			Sticks or tubs of clay
			Paper towels
Retailers:	All materials can be purchased online or from small businesses or large chain retailers.		

Setup Instructions for

Clay Boat

The Boat

1. Get clay sticks or tubs of clay for participants to mold into boats.
2. If this will be a make-and-take station, be sure to have enough clay for each participant.

The Waterway

1. Use clear plastic containers or bowls.
2. Fill each bowl or container with water to use as the waterway in which the boats will float.
3. Have paper towels available for participants to use in case of spills.

The Weights

1. Gather pennies, paper clips, binder rings, or any other lightweight objects participants can place in their boats to determine capacity.
2. Sort the objects, and place each group in a container.

Display

Set out the Family Fun Card, clay, water-filled containers, paper towels, containers of weights, and books (optional) related to capacity, buoyancy, floating, etc.

Optional: Set up a small swimming pool for participants to test and float their boats together.

Cover Your Bases

Family Fun Card

What happens when you mix cooking spices with household chemicals?

Explore:

1. Put on safety glasses to protect your eyes.
2. Add ½ teaspoon turmeric to ¼ cup rubbing alcohol.
3. Add ¼ teaspoon baking soda to ¼ cup water.
4. Add drops of the turmeric mixture to the baking soda mixture until you see a reaction happen (Hint: a new color).
5. Now, add drops of vinegar to the baking soda mixture from Step 3 until you see a reaction happen.

Bonus: Use litmus paper to figure out which liquid is an acid and which is a base.

1. Dip litmus papers into the baking soda mixture, the turmeric mixture, and the vinegar; then wait for the papers to change color.
2. Use a litmus chart to see if the paper turns color for an acid or a base.

Cover Your Bases

Family Fun Card

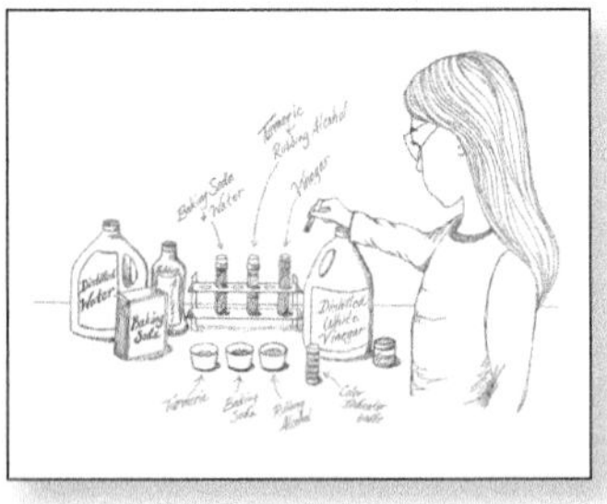

Expected Result:

You should see the turmeric mixture turn red when it mixes with the baking soda mixture. The turmeric–baking soda mixture should turn yellow again and get bubbly when the vinegar mixture is added to it.

The litmus paper should become a color that matches a pH between 0 and 6 for the vinegar and the turmeric mixture and a pH between 8 and 14 for the baking soda mixture.

Explanation:

Turmeric is an ordinary kitchen spice that is an acid—a chemical that has extra hydrogen molecules to give away. Baking soda is a base—a chemical that has extra pairs of hydrogen and oxygen molecules to give away. Vinegar is also an acid.

When the turmeric mixture turned from yellow to red, it was changing from an acid to a base. The mixture turned back to yellow after you added vinegar because it was changing from a base back to an acid.

Litmus paper turns different colors in different types of liquids. The color it turns depends on the number of hydrogen molecules in the liquid. The paper will become a reddish color with acids and a bluish color with bases.

Experience More at Home:

Use litmus paper to discover the acids and bases you have in your home. You can buy litmus paper online or from your local pharmacy.

The Organizer's Checklist for
Cover Your Bases

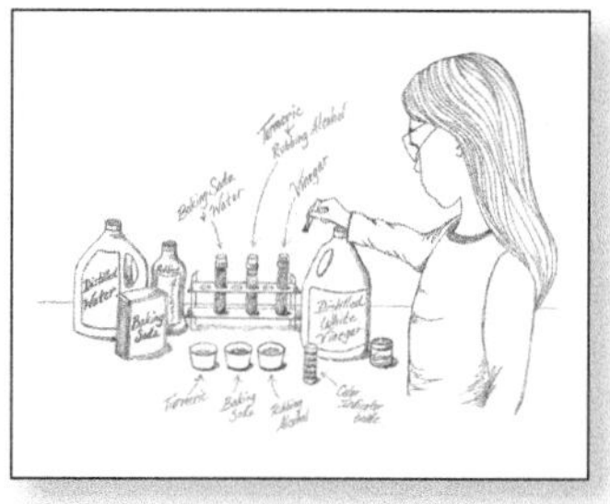

Station Checklist			
Materials:	Reusable		Safety glasses
			Test tubes with tops and test tube racks
			Measuring spoons
			Measuring cups
			Lidded cups or containers (to hold the dry and wet ingredients)
			Cups (to stand pipettes in)
			Foil pan or plastic bin to dump used liquids
			Plastic funnels
	Consumable		Garbage bags
			Masking tape or duct tape
			Distilled water
			Rubbing alcohol
			Vinegar
			Baking soda
			Turmeric
			Plastic, disposable pipettes
			Litmus paper (also called pH paper)
			Paper towels
	Safety		MSDS for rubbing alcohol
			MSDS for vinegar
			MSDS for turmeric
			MSDS for baking soda

(continued)

Retailers:	Plastic, disposable pipettes can be purchased from Steve Spangler Science (www.stevespanglerscience.com), Science Bob (www.sciencebob.com), and Amazon (www.amazon.com). Safety glasses can be ordered from Staples (www.staples.com), Lakeshore Learning Store (www.lakeshorelearning.com), and Amazon (www.amazon.com). Test tubes with tops, called "baby soda bottles," can be purchased from Steve Spangler Science (www.stevespanglerscience.com), Educational Innovations (www.teachersource.com) as "soda bottle preforms and caps," and from Amazon (www.amazon.com) as "plastic test tubes with caps." Material safety data sheets (MSDS) can be found online for rubbing alcohol, vinegar, turmeric, and baking soda.

Setup Instructions for
Cover Your Bases

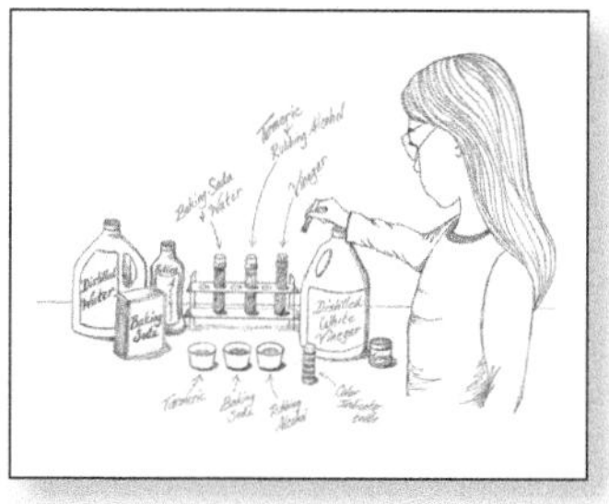

Note: You will find it helpful to run this station with at least three station hosts, especially if you plan to have at least two sets going at once.

Acids and Bases

1. Cover the table with plastic garbage bags, and tape them down, since turmeric can stain light-colored areas.
2. Label and fill the three test tubes: "Baking Soda and Water," "Turmeric and Rubbing Alcohol," and "Vinegar." Place them in the test tube rack.
3. Sit the test tube racks in foil pans with funnels next to them so participants can easily pour liquids into them.
4. Put the measuring spoons and cups on the table for hosts to guide participants through making measurements or for families to do it on their own.
5. Have the baking soda and turmeric in labeled and lidded containers that are easy for young participants to scoop from with assistance.
6. Put cups filled with plastic pipettes on the table for participants to add drops of the turmeric mixture to the baking soda mixture and to add drops of the vinegar to the baking soda mixture.
7. Have an empty plastic bin or foil pan ready for participants to dump the baking soda and turmeric mixtures into when finished.
8. Have paper towels (or paper plates) ready for participants to set wet and used litmus paper strips on after using them to test the pH of the baking soda mixture, turmeric mixture, and vinegar.

Display

Place the safety glasses and Family Fun Card on the station table. Set the labeled and capped test tubes in their racks and the measuring cups and measuring spoons in front.

Have the cup(s) of plastic pipettes, baking soda, turmeric, vinegar, rubbing alcohol, and water near the test tubes. Set the empty bin or pan on the table close to the test tubes so participants can easily dump the mixtures.

Crazy Worm

Family Fun Card

What kind of polymer "worm" will you make?

Explore:

NOTE: Crazy worm materials can irritate the eyes. Be sure to wash your hands after this activity.

1. Squirt a little bit of "Worm Goo" into the "Worm Activator."
2. What did you see form? Tell a friend next to you.
3. Pull the "worm" out of the activator with a spoon or your fingers.
4. Squeeze it. What does it feel like? What does it look like?
5. Write a short story or poem about or illustrate (draw pictures) to show a day in the life of your worm, or just tell the story out loud.
6. Share your written or spoken story, poem, or illustrations with a friend.

Crazy Worm

Family Fun Card

Expected Result:

You should see a stringy "worm" form as you squirt "Worm Goo" into the "Worm Activator." The "worm" is a polymer, a substance that can act a little bit like a solid and a little bit like a liquid at the same time.

Explanation:

Worm Goo is made from sodium alginate, which is a substance that's taken from algae to thicken foods such as ice cream and pie fillings. The activator has lots of calcium in it. When the sodium alginate and calcium mix together, they make something called a polymer—something that's a liquid and a solid at the same time. The worm is somewhat hard on the outside and somewhat soft and squishy inside.

Experience More at Home:

Read the nutrition labels of dairy products, ice cream, sauces, gravies, and pie fillings to see if they have sodium alginate.

Go to www.livestrong.com/article/264769-foods-with-sodium-alginate to read about foods that have sodium alginate and other products that are made with it.

The Organizer's Checklist for
Crazy Worm

Station Checklist			
Materials:	Reusable		Squirt bottles and plastic cups
			Plastic spoons
			Permanent markers (e.g., Sharpies)
			Large plastic bottle that can hold up to 1 gallon of water
			Fiction or nonfiction books about worms (optional)
	Consumable		Crazy Worm (sold as Insta Worm)
			Water
			Plastic sandwich bags
	Safety		MSDS for Worm Goo
			MSDS for Worm Activator
Retailers:	Insta Worm kits and refills can be purchased from Steve Spangler Science (www.stevespanglerscience.com), Amazon (www.amazon.com), or small businesses. Material safety data sheets (MSDS) can be found by doing an Internet search with keywords "MSDS for Worm Goo" and "MSDS for Worm Activator." All other materials can be purchased online or from small businesses or large chain retailers.		

Setup Instructions for

Crazy Worm

Worm Goo and Activator

1. Label squirt bottle(s) "Worm Goo."
2. Label clear plastic cup(s) "Worm Activator."
3. Prepare the Worm Goo and Worm Activator according to package directions.
4. Pour the Worm Goo and Worm Activator into the appropriately labeled bottles or cups.
5. Follow the instructions on the Family Fun Card to make a test worm.

Display

1. Put the Family Fun Card, squirt bottle(s) filled with Worm Goo, plastic cup(s) filled with Worm Activator, plastic spoon(s), permanent markers, and plastic bags on display.
2. Put a sample plastic bag with your name on it and a Crazy Worm inside to show how worms should be taken home.
3. **Optional:** Display a fiction or nonfiction book about worms, and encourage participants to write and illustrate their own stories about their worms' first day at home with them.
4. **Optional:** Display polymers and non-polymers to sort and compare.

Tip for Crazy Worm

You can vary this activity by adding a few drops of food coloring to each bottle of Worm Goo. Use one squirt bottle for each color of Worm Goo you make.

Fingerprint ID

Family Fun Card

What kind of Type 14 fingerprint pattern do you have?

Explore:

1. Make what the Federal Bureau of Investigation (FBI) calls a Type 14 Flat Impression.
    a. Write your name on a fingerprint card.
    b. Lightly tap (without rolling) the four fingers of your left and right hands on the ink pad and gently touch them on the card. Next, lightly tap your thumbs on the pad and touch them on the cards.
2. Use the magnifying glass to look closely at your fingerprint. Put a small dot in the center of it.
3. Compare your fingerprint with the ones that are on the ID card. What kind of fingerprint do you have?
4. Now, make a fingerprint on the "Gallery of Prints," and compare your prints to the prints others have made.

Fingerprint ID

Family Fun Card

Expected Result:

You should be able to make what the FBI calls a Type 14 Flat Impression. You should then be able to compare your fingerprint to those you see on the fingerprint ID card.

Explanation:

A fingerprint is a print that comes from the ridges on your fingers. Everyone has a unique fingerprint, even twins! We naturally leave fingerprints on surfaces we touch because our skin makes oil. It's like having your own pad of invisible ink. A Type 14 Flat Impression is a kind of fingerprint that police officers and investigators use to make the most accurate copy of someone's fingerprint. It is called a "flat" impression because you make this kind of print by flattening, or tapping, your fingers on the paper instead of rolling them onto the paper.

Experience More at Home:

Did you know the FBI collects about 13,000 fingerprints each day? Go to www.fbi.gov/about-us/cjis/fingerprints_biometrics/recording-legible-fingerprints/takingfps to read about the national database the FBI is making.

The Organizer's Checklist for

Fingerprint ID

Station Checklist			
Materials:	Reusable		Washable ink
			Magnifying glasses
			Pencils
			Sample fingerprint card
			Fingerprint pattern type card
	Consumable		Copy paper (½ sheet), large index cards, or fingerprint record cards downloaded from the Internet
			Baby wipes
			Poster board or paper (for the "Gallery of Prints")
	Safety		MSDS for washable ink
Retailers:	Fingerprint pattern type cards and examples of how to take the best-quality fingerprints can be found on the Federal Bureau of Investigation (FBI) Web site (www.fbi.gov). Enter the keywords "fingerprint pattern type" in the search field to find the name and picture of each type of fingerprint a person may have. Enter the terms "capturing legible fingerprints" in the search field to find examples of quality fingerprints as a pdf. The material safety data sheet (MSDS) for washable ink can be found by doing an Internet search with keywords "MSDS for washable ink." All other materials can be purchased online or from small businesses or large chain retailers.		

Setup Instructions for
Fingerprint ID

Fingerprint Pattern Type Cards

Print and cold laminate (optional) fingerprint pattern type cards, showing pictures for loops, arches, double loops, etc.

Making Fingerprints

1. Have available ½ sheets of copy paper, index cards, or fingerprint record cards.
2. Set the washable ink, magnifying glasses, pencils, and baby wipes near the fingerprint record cards.

Display Area

Set the magnifying glasses, fingerprint record cards, fingerprint pattern type cards, washable ink, pencils, baby wipes, and Family Fun Card in close proximity to one another and in plain sight on the table for participants to see. Prepare a poster or paper labeled "Gallery of Prints," and hang it on the wall or set it on the table for all participants to add a fingerprint.

Fishing for Planets

Family Fun Card

Which planets will you catch?

Explore:

1. Hold the magnetic end of the pole over the planet you want to catch until it touches the magnet on a planet.
2. Catch three planets.
3. Which of the eight planets did you catch? Which is closest to the sun? Which is farthest from the sun?

Fishing for Planets

Family Fun Card

Expected Result:

You should be able to catch the planets by touching the magnetic end of a pole to the magnetic side of the planets. You should also be able to name the planets you caught and use information to put them in order from closest to the sun to farthest from the sun.

Explanation:

The positive and negative ends of magnets attract each other. When they touch, they stick together! The order of the eight planets from our sun is Mercury, Venus, Earth, Mars, Jupiter, Saturn, Uranus, and Neptune.

Experience More at Home:

Go to http://photojournal.jpl.nasa.gov/ from NASA to see color photos of each planet.

Want a fun way to remember the planets in our solar system? Watch the Little Einstein's "Race to the Planet" episode, or order it online.

Use this fun sentence to memorize the order of the eight planets from the sun: My Very Excited Mom Just Sat Under Neptune (Mercury, Venus, Earth, Mars, Jupiter, Saturn, Uranus, Neptune)

The Organizer's Checklist for **Fishing for Planets**

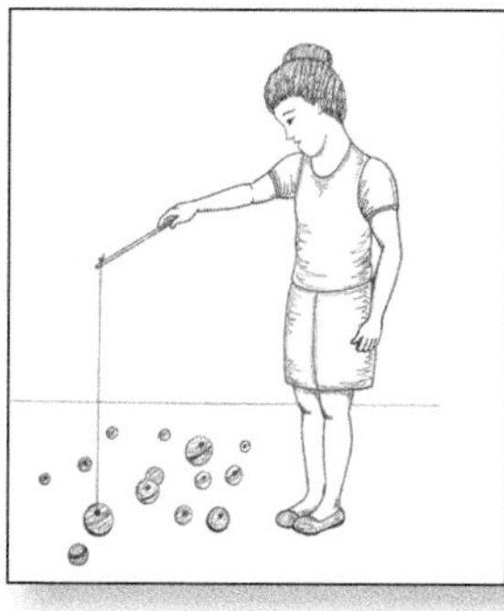

Station Checklist			
Materials:	Reusable		(Laminated) pictures of planets
			Wooden dowel rod
			Magnetic strips
			Books or other resources on planets or write info on the back of the planets
			Small inflatable or plastic pool or other item to contain spills
	Consumable		Yarn, string, or fishing line
			Tape or glue to adhere magnets & planets
Retailers:	Local craft stores, small businesses, or large chain retailers		

Setup Instructions for

Fishing for Planets

The Fishing Pole

1. Cut a piece of yarn, string, or fishing line to the length you desire.
2. Attach it to the wooden dowel with tape, glue, or a knot.
3. Attach a magnetic strip to the end of the line.

The Planet Pool

Get an inflatable swimming pool, a hat, a bin, or another container in which you can place the planets. Attach magnetic strips to the backs of the laminated planets.

Display

Put the planets in the planet pool. Lay the fishing poles next to the pool or drape them over the side of it. Set out the Family Fun Card and the books, posters, computers, or other resources participants can use to learn more about the planets they catch or write information on the back of each planet.

Floating Balls

Family Fun Card

What scientific principle makes airplanes float in the air?

Explore:

1. Turn on the blow-dryer (with an adult).
2. Put a plastic ball in the dryer's stream of air.
3. Does the ball float in the air or shoot up to the ceiling?
4. Add a second ball. Do both balls float or do they fly away?
5. Tilt the dryer; see how far it can tilt before the balls fall.

Floating Balls

Family Fun Card

Expected Result:

You should see the plastic ball(s) rise in the stream of air for a moment, then slow down to balance in the air. The same principle that explains why a ball balances in the air explains how airplanes balance in the sky.

Explanation:

What keeps the ball from moving up and down so much?

It's Bernoulli's (ber-nu-leez) principle! The stream of air from the hair dryer pushes the ball up until its force matches the strength of gravity pulling down so the ball becomes balanced. It's the same principle that shows why airplanes can fly!

What keeps the ball from moving side to side so much?

Bernoulli's principle says when a force (such as a blow-dryer) makes air speed up past an object, the air doesn't have much time to "press" on the object. This weak push from the fast-moving air is called low air pressure. It is much weaker than the high air pressure from the slow-moving air around it. The balanced force of low and high air pressure keeps the ball still.

Experience More at Home:

Search www.ehow.com with the keywords "Bernoulli's Principle" to see videos and more at-home projects about this very cool scientific principle.

The Organizer's Checklist for

Floating Balls

Station Checklist			
Materials:	Reusable		Blow-dryers (2)
			Extension cords (2)
			Small plastic 40 mm or other lightweight plastic balls
			Plastic bins (2)
			Newspaper, cotton, scrap paper, towels, or brown bags (to line bins and prevent balls from bouncing away)
	Consumable		NONE
Retailers:	Small businesses or large chain retailers		

Setup Instructions for

Floating Balls

The Blow-Dryers and Balls

1. Get hand-held hair dryers to float balls in the air.
2. Have extension cords available in case the outlets needed to power the dryers are far away.
3. Have several plastic balls available for participants to place into the stream of air coming from the hand-held hair dryers. Small, plastic, 40 mm balls tend to work best.
4. Have multiple sets of plastic balls available in case some roll away and get lost.
5. Have containers available to hold each set of balls.

The "Catcher"

1. Have one plastic bin or cardboard box available to "catch" the balls for each hair dryer.
2. Line the plastic bin or cardboard box with newspaper or similar material that can absorb the impact and prevent the balls from bouncing away.

Display

Set the hair dryers, plastic "catcher" bins lined with paper or other absorbent material, containers filled plastic balls, and Family Fun Card out for participants to use.

Fossil Hunt

Family Fun Card

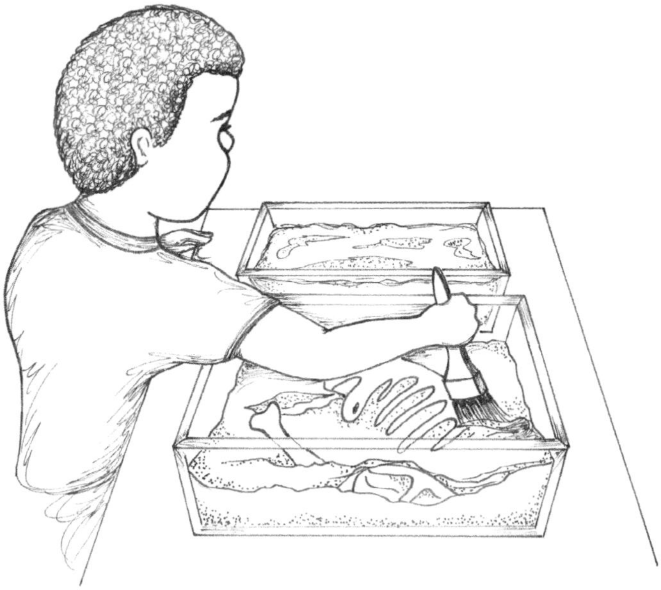

What body and trace fossils will you find?

Explore:

1. Choose the paleontologist tools you want to use: a brush, an apron, a shovel, a magnifying glass, or gloves.
2. Find two types of fossils:
   a. **Body fossils:** parts that used to be part of the animal's body, such as teeth, bones, and arms
   b. **Trace fossils:** "stuff" and prints animals leave behind, such as footprints, tooth marks, skin, nests, eggs, and poop (yes … poop!).
3. Sort your body fossils and trace fossils. How many of each kind of fossil do you see?

Bonus: Choose a body fossil to make a print using wax paper and clay. Wrap the wax paper around the fossil and gently press it into the clay until you make a print.

Fossil Hunt

Family Fun Card

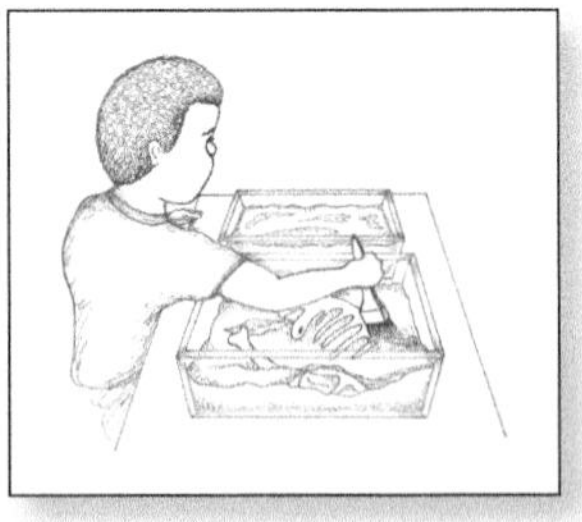

Expected Result:

You should be able to identify and sort two types of fossils: body fossils and trace fossils.

Explanation:

The word *fossil* means "dug up." Fossils are clues that have been left behind by plants and animals. Fossils tell us where plants and animals lived, how they behaved, what they looked like, and much, much more!

Experience More at Home:

Visit the Enchanted Learning Web site at www.enchantedlearning.com to learn about famous fossil hunters.

The Organizer's Checklist for

Fossil Hunt

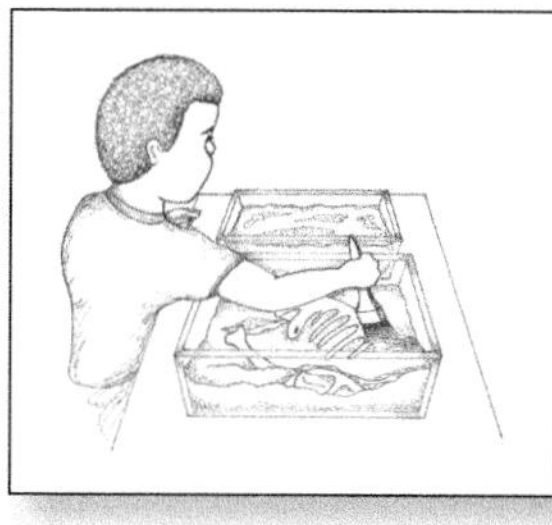

Station Checklist			
Materials:	Reusable		Shallow plastic bins or foil pans
			Sand, rice, or corn kernels to bury fossils in
			Aprons, shovels, gloves for participants to use as they explore the fossils
			Fossils
			Identification cards
			Magnifying glass
			Paintbrushes
			Sorting bins, mats, or plates
			Safety glasses (optional)
			Fossil rubbing plates
			Resource books (optional)
	Consumable		Labels
			Paper
			Crayons
			Tape (optional)
			Pencils
Retailers:	Fossil kits and sorting collections can be ordered online from Educational Fossils (www.educationalfossils.com), Educational Innovations (www.teachersource.com), and Amazon (www.amazon.com). Other retailers can be found by doing an Internet search with keywords "fossil kits." Fossil rubbing plates can be purchased from Acorn Naturalists (www.acornnaturalists.com), Amazon (www.amazon.com), and Science Kit (sciencekit.com). Other retailers can be found through an Internet search with the keywords "fossil rubbing plates." Safety glasses can be ordered from Staples (www.staples.com), Lakeshore Learning Store (www.lakeshorelearning.com), and Amazon (www.amazon.com). Other retailers can be found through an Internet search with keywords "safety glasses for kids." The remaining materials can be purchased from small businesses, large chain retailers, or craft stores.		

Setup Instructions for
Fossil Hunt

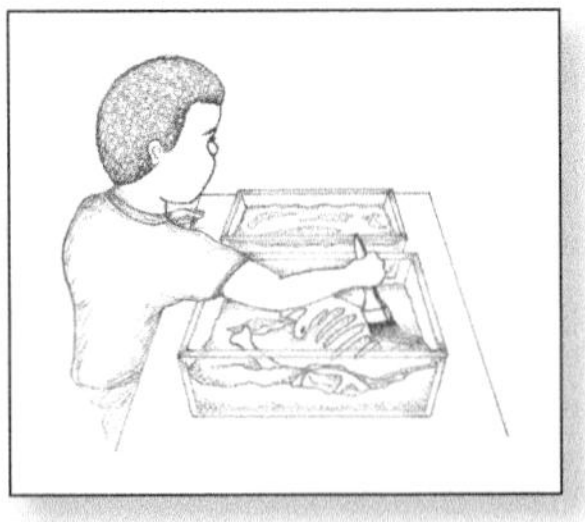

Fossil Digging Area

1. Fill shallow plastic bins or foil pans with sand, rice, or corn kernels.
2. Scatter the fossils in the sand.
3. Prepare identification cards to match each fossil participants will find, or set out the cards that came with fossils if they are available.
4. Have magnifying glasses; paintbrushes; sorting bins, mats, or plates; identification cards; and safety glasses (optional) at the digging area.
5. Have books available for participants to learn more about each fossil they will find (optional).

Fossil Rubbing Plates

1. Get fossil rubbing plates, paper, crayons, and tape (optional).
2. Label each rubbing plate with the name of the fossil(s).
3. Prepare a sample rubbing of one or more of the plates.
4. Have books available for participants to learn more about each fossil shown on the rubbing plates (optional).

Tips for the Fossil Hunt

The best types of fossil kits to purchase when catering to a large crowd are kits with many different types of fossils and identification cards that include large pictures of and information about the fossils.

Display

Set out the fossil digging area, rubbing plates, books, and Family Fun Card close to one another. Ensure that the materials for the digging area and the fossil rubbings are in plain sight for participants.

Germ Glow

Family Fun Card

Where can germs hide on your hands?

Explore:

1. Put your hands under the black light. Are they glowing?
2. Squirt one pump of "germ lotion" onto your hands, and look at them under the black light again.
3. Notice all the spots on your hands that are glowing.
4. The glowing spots on your hands are all the places where germs can hide.
5. Wash your hands with soap by rubbing your palms, the back of your hands, in between your fingers, and under your nails.
6. Remember to moisturize, too, so you can fill in the cracks where germs can hide! This will help keep them out.

Germ Glow

Family Fun Card

Expected Result:

You should be able to see the spaces on your hands where germs can hide.

Explanation:

The germ lotion has tiny particles in it that are activated by ultraviolet (UV), or black, light. These UV particles glow when your hands are in black light.

Experience More at Home:

Learn about good hand-washing techniques from the Centers for Disease Control and Prevention at www.cdc.gov/handwashing.

The Organizer's Checklist for
Germ Glow

Station Checklist			
Materials:	Reusable		Black light (long-wave ultraviolet light)
			Black light stand
			Extension cord
	Consumable		Glitter Bug Lotion or Glo Germ (an optional alternative is cinnamon and petroleum jelly)
			Hand sanitizer
			Baby wipes
			Lotion or petroleum jelly
	Safety		MSDS for Glitter Bug or Glo Germ lotion
Retailers:	Glitter Bug Lotion can be purchased from Steve Spangler Science (www.stevespanglerscience.com). Glo Germ can be purchased from Educational Innovations (www.teachersource.com). Long black (long-wave ultraviolet) lights and stands can be purchased from Educational Innovations (www.teachersource.com). Black lights can also be purchased from Edmund Scientifics (www.scientificsonline.com) and Amazon (www.amazon.com). Material safety data sheets (MSDS) can be found by doing an Internet search using the keywords "MSDS for Glitter Bug Lotion" or "Glo Germ." The remaining materials can be purchased from small businesses or large chain retailers.		

Setup Instructions for

Germ Glow

The Black Light

1. Get a long-wave black light for participants to put their hands under.
2. Have an extension cord available to plug it in.

The Germ Lotion

1. Have several bottles of the germ lotion available for participants.
2. Plan for participants to use at least one squirt each.
3. Have hand sanitizer or baby wipes for participants to wipe the germ lotion off their hands if a sink is not available for hand washing.

Optional: As an alternative to germ lotion, have participants rub a small amount of petroleum jelly on their hands, then sprinkle them with cinnamon and shake hands with a family member or friend who does not have cinnamon on their hands. The goal is for young participants to relate the cinnamon to germs and to understand that when they touch someone else's hands, they will share germs.

Tips for Black Light

Use a black light that is enclosed in a table-top stand, as shown in the illustration, so participants' eyes will be protected from the light while they visualize the cracks in their hands where germs can hide.

Display

Put the black light, germ lotion, hand sanitizer or baby wipes, Family Fun Card, and lotion (optional) on display for participants.

Marker Magic

Family Fun Card

How can permanent markers and rubbing alcohol create tie-dye?

Explore:

1. Use permanent marker to color a 1-inch to 2-inch pattern in the center of the cotton fabric.
2. Use a rubber band to fix the cotton material to the open end of a cup. Make sure the pattern you colored is in the middle.
3. Use a pipette to slowly squeeze rubbing alcohol on your pattern until the colors spread as far as you want.
4. Give your pattern time to dry.

Marker Magic

Family Fun Card

Expected Result:

You should see the permanent marker pattern spread across the cotton material as you add drops of rubbing alcohol to it.

Explanation:

The ink from a permanent marker soaks into cotton material. As the rubbing alcohol passes over the ink, the ink is lifted off the pattern you made and is carried across the material until the alcohol stops.

Experience More at Home:

Wash the tie-dye pattern you made in different detergents to see if it is permanent.

Try making patterns with different brands of markers on different materials to see which work best.

The Organizer's Checklist for
Marker Magic

Station Checklist			
Materials:	Reusable		Scissors
			Plastic cups or test tubes and test tube racks
			Rubber bands
			Permanent markers (e.g., Sharpies)
			Sample Marker Magic square
	Consumable		Cotton T-shirts (cut into squares)
			Masking tape
			Plastic, disposable pipettes
			Rubbing alcohol
			Plastic garbage bags
			Magic Eraser (or similar)
	Safety		MSDS for rubbing alcohol
Retailers:	Plastic, disposable pipettes can be purchased from Steve Spangler Science (www.stevespanglerscience.com), Science Bob (www.sciencebob.com), and Amazon (www.amazon.com). They can also be found online by doing an Internet search with keywords "plastic pipette Cartesian." Material safety data sheets (MSDS) can be found by doing an Internet search with keywords "MSDS for rubbing alcohol." All other materials can be purchased online or from small businesses or large chain retailers.		

Setup Instructions for

Marker Magic

Cotton Squares

1. Get enough cotton squares for each participant to make a tie-dye.
2. Cut the squares to a size that is large enough to cover the opening of the cup to which they will fasten it.
3. Get masking tape for participants to write their names on the cotton fabric.

Tie-Dye "Stands"

1. Get cups for participants to use as "stands."
2. The cotton squares will be attached to the stand with rubber bands.

The Marker Magic Square

1. Cover the table with plastic garbage bags, and tape them down.
2. Get markers, pipettes, rubbing alcohol, and plastic cups or test tubes for participants to use to do their "marker magic."
3. Pour the rubbing alcohol into the plastic cups or test tubes.
4. Place the pipettes in the test tubes for participants to use to drop the alcohol onto their cotton fabric.
5. Use Magic Eraser and rubbing alcohol to clean the tables if permanent marker stains them.

Display

Set out the test tubes filled with rubbing alcohol, cotton squares, pipettes, masking tape, permanent markers, and a sample Marker Magic square for participants. Display the Family Fun Card with it.

Mobile Planetarium

Family Fun Card

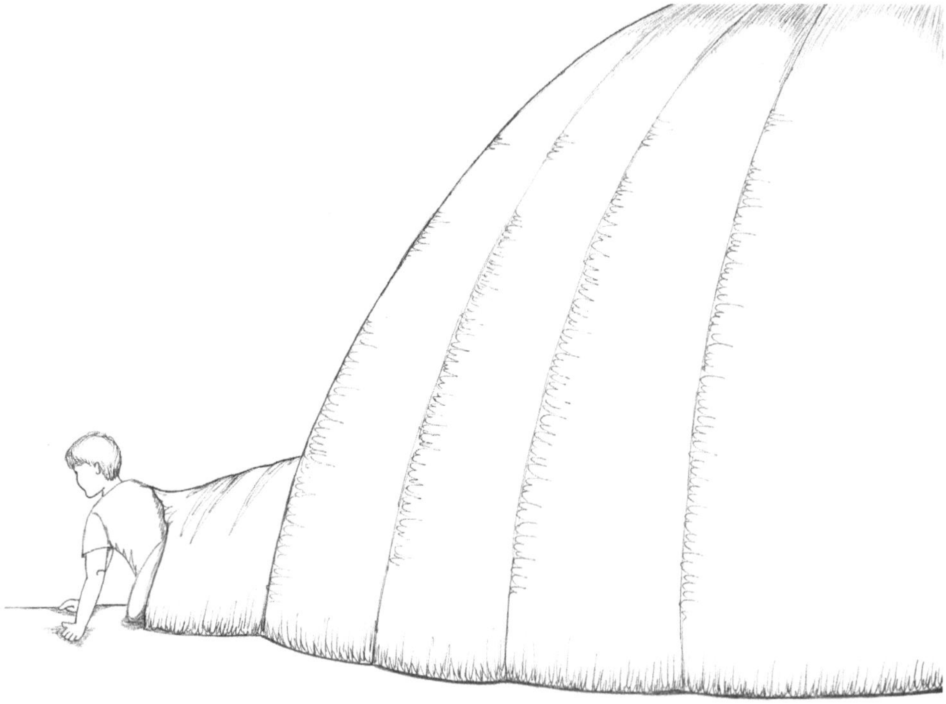

What can you learn about the heavens and our solar system?

Explore:

1. Enter the mobile planetarium when it's your turn.
2. Listen to the presentation.
3. Think of one question you can ask the planetarium speaker.
4. Listen for the names of constellations, planets, stars, and more fun facts from the field of astronomy.
5. After the presentation, draw a picture that shows the constellations or planets you enjoyed.
6. Draw your own unique constellation. Write a story that names the constellation and how it got its name.

Mobile Planetarium

Family Fun Card

Expected Result:

You should become familiar with the planets in our solar system and the constellations made up of stars from outside our solar system.

Experience More at Home:

Check out National Geographic's "cosmic neighborhood" at http://science.nationalgeographic.com/science/space/solar-system/ to learn fun facts about outer space.

Visit National Geographic's Photo Gallery: Solar System at science.nationalgeographic.com/science/photos/solar-system-gallery/#/jupiter-by-hubble_1019_600x450.jpg to see color pictures of the planets in our solar system.

The Organizer's Checklist for

Mobile Planetarium

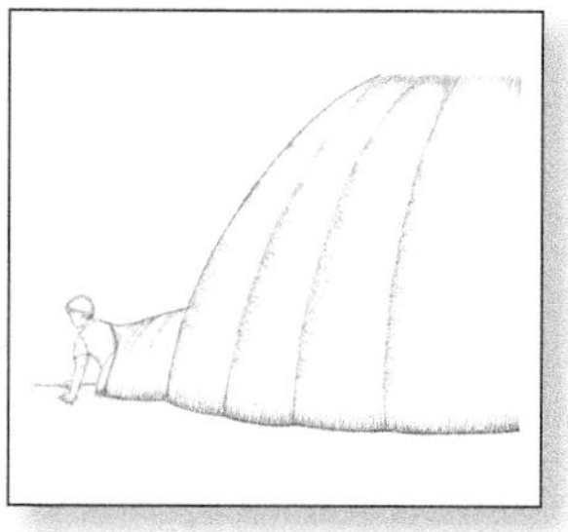

Station Checklist			
Materials:	Reusable		Portable microphone and speaker (optional)
			Crayons
			Mobile planetarium (rented from a provider)
	Consumable		Paper
Retailers:	Mobile planetariums can be reserved from Mobile Ed (www.mobile edproductions.com). They may also be rented from some museums, small businesses, or providers of educational programming.		

Setup Instructions for

Mobile Planetarium

Planetarium

1. The best place to set up a mobile planetarium is in a gymnasium.
2. Locate a power outlet into which the vendor can plug the planetarium, and identify a place where the planetarium will be inflated.
3. The vendor you hire should inflate the planetarium and share pertinent details with you.
4. Consider having a portable microphone and speaker available for the vendor to use. You will find the microphone to be particularly beneficial if other stations, besides the mobile planetarium, will be set up in the gymnasium, since the sounds of families engaging in the other stations may make it difficult to hear the planetarium presentation without a microphone.

Tips for the Planetarium

If the mobile planetarium program will be run several times during your event (every 45 minutes, for example), consider having families sign up for particular time slots to balance out the number of families that will attend mobile planetarium presentations at one time.

Display

Set out the Family Fun Card, sign-up sheets (optional), crayons, and paper in plain sight for participants to see and use.

Move to the Beat

Family Fun Card

What's the difference between your resting heart rate and your active heart rate?

Explore:

NOTE: This station must be operated by an adult, preferably a nurse or doctor.

1. Use the digital stethoscope and battery-powered speakers to listen to your heartbeat while you are sitting or standing still.
2. Count the number of beats you hear in 30 seconds. Write down the number. This is your resting heart rate.
3. Move to the beat of music, play jump rope, or do jumping jacks for 30 seconds.
4. Use the digital stethoscope and battery-powered speakers to listen to your heartbeat again.
5. Count the number of beats you hear in 30 seconds. Write down the number. This is your active heart rate.
6. What's the difference between your active and resting heart rates?

Move to the Beat

Family Fun Card

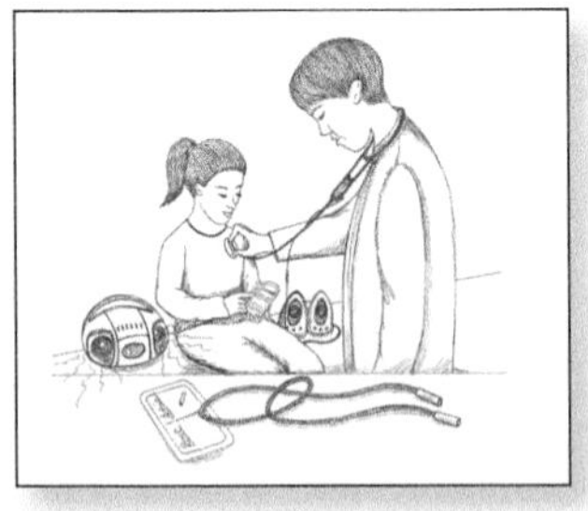

Expected Result:

You should be able to use the digital stethoscope to discover your resting and active heart rates.

Explanation:

Digital stethoscopes are electronic devices that can be attached to battery-powered speakers so one or more heart rates can be heard out loud. They are often used as teaching tools for doctors or nurses. For elementary students, digital stethoscopes are a great tool to use to demonstrate the positive difference physical exercise can have on the resting heart rate.

Experience More at Home:

Visit www.letsmove.gov to see how you can move with your family to the beat of your heart through physical exercise!

The Organizer's Checklist for

Move to the Beat

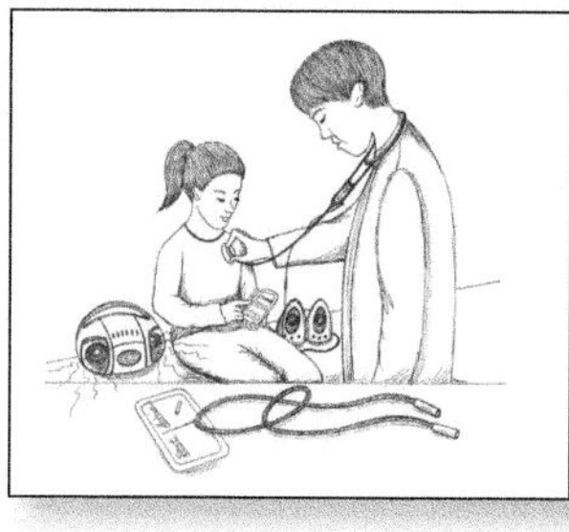

Station Checklist			
Materials:	Reusable		Digital stethoscope
			Battery-operated speakers
			Batteries for the digital stethoscope, speakers, and music player (as needed)
			Chalkboard with chalk (or chart paper with markers or index cards with crayons)
			Jump rope (or other athletic equipment participants can use to get their heart rates up)
			Music player
			Timer
			Books relating to exercise (optional)
	Consumable		Hand sanitizer
Retailers:	Digital stethoscopes can be purchased from All Heart (www.allheart.com) or Amazon (www.amazon.com). You can also find them by doing an Internet search with keywords "digital stethoscopes." All other materials can be purchased online or from small businesses or large chain retailers.		

Setup Instructions for

Move to the Beat

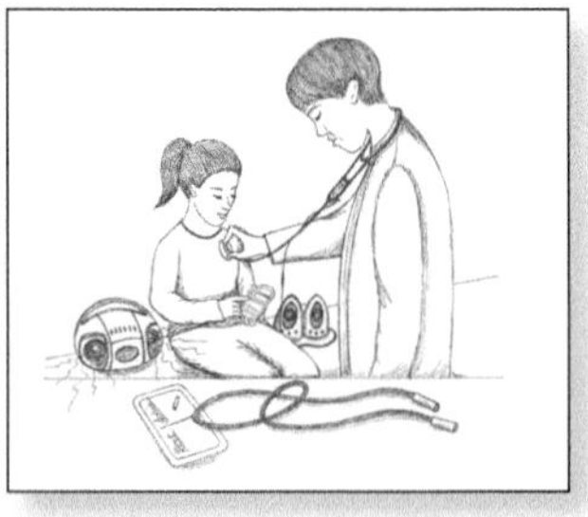

Digital Stethoscope and Battery-Operated Speakers

1. The best place to host this activity is in a room where the heartbeats can actually be heard. A classroom is usually a great location. Remember to caution participants that A PARENT/GUARDIAN OR A MEDICAL PROFESSIONAL should use the digital stethoscope according to the manufacturer's directions. Digital stethoscopes can BE USED ONLY WITH BATTERY-OPERATED SPEAKERS. Otherwise, participants may get an electric shock when the stethoscope is held over the heart.
2. You may want to put tape over the earpieces of the digital stethoscope, so parents remember that they should not insert the earpieces into their ears, to minimize the spread of germs.
3. Set out hand sanitizer for use before trying the stethoscope.
4. Have a member of your team available to answer questions about the stethoscope and to ensure that parents or guardians use only the battery-operated speakers to amplify the heartbeat.

Moving to the Beat

Set up the music player near an electrical outlet, or have enough batteries.

Display

Set up the music player, jump rope (or other athletic equipment to increase heart rate), chalkboard with chalk (or chart paper with markers or index cards with crayons), digital stethoscope with taped earpieces, timer, and Family Fun Card.

Paint a Mold

Family Fun Card

Which animal tracks can you find?

Explore:

1. Use the scientific tools to look closely at the animal tracks.
2. Tell a friend what you notice about the nails, toes, or claws, and the size of the tracks.
3. Have you seen these tracks outside before? Match the track with the picture of the animal that made it.

Now, let's paint an animal track mold you can keep!

1. Choose the animal track mold you want to paint.
2. Write your name on the bottom of the mold.
3. Paint the mold and set it aside to dry.

Paint a Mold

Family Fun Card

Expected Result:

You should be able to match the animal track mold with the picture of the animal that made the tracks and identify the animal track for each rubbing in the nature walk booklet.

Experience More at Home:

Watch the YouTube video titled "Common Animal Tracks," presented by a Naturalist from the State University of New York, to learn what to look for when searching for animal tracks in the snow.

The Organizer's Checklist for **Paint a Mold**

Station Checklist			
Materials:	Reusable		Rubber animal track molds
			Paintbrushes
			Books and pictures relating to animals or animal tracks (optional)
			Permanent markers
			Shallow tinfoil pan with a thin layer of Play-Doh, clay, sand, or flour that has been imprinted with an animal track
	Consumable		Plaster of paris
			Paint
			Cups
			Newspaper or plastic to protect work space
Retailers:	Rubber animal track molds can be purchased from Acorn Naturalists (www.acornnaturalists.com) or Ward's Natural Science (www.wardsci.com).		

Setup Instructions for

Paint a Mold

Making the Molds

1. At least one day BEFORE the event, prepare plaster of paris according to package directions.
2. Rub the rubber mold with petroleum jelly before pouring the plaster in it.
3. Pour plaster into each rubber mold.
4. Gently tap the sides of the rubber mold just after pouring the plaster inside so any air bubbles will be released.
5. Allow it to harden.
6. Carefully remove each mold from the rubber once hardened.
7. If you have to transport the molds, wrap them in paper towels to prevent them from cracking.

Painting the Molds

1. Get paper, paintbrushes, paints, newspaper, and masking tape.
2. Designate an area for participants to paint their molds and to set them out to dry.
3. Cover the area with newspaper or plastic.

Connecting to Literacy

Get story or informational books about animal tracks for participants to use.

Display

Set out the Family Fun Card, animal track molds, paints, paintbrushes, newspaper, tape, permanent markers, and books (optional) for participants to use.

Paper Airplane

Family Fun Card

How fast or slow is your plane, and how far can it travel?

Explore:

1. Design a paper airplane using a template, or use your own design. You can design your plane to be fast or slow—you choose!
2. Stand at the tarmac and get ready to fly your plane.
3. Ask an adult or a friend to start the timer when your plane takes off and stop it when it lands.
4. Use chalk, a marker, or a pencil to mark where your plane lands on the tarmac.
5. Discover the speed of your plane by dividing the distance it flew by the time it took to land.

For groups of three or more:

Choose a pilot to fly the plane, a timekeeper to see how long it takes the plane to land, and a recorder to mark where the plane lands.

Paper Airplane

Family Fun Card

Expected Result:

You should be able to design a paper airplane, see that some designs fly faster or slower than others, and calculate the speed of your paper airplane and how far it traveled.

Explanation:

When you throw a paper airplane, the air below its wings pushes the plane up so it can stay in the air. The plane flies the farthest when it is lightweight and when the wings are curved in a way that air passes quickly over the top and slowly on the bottom. This helps the plane stay in the air as long as possible.

Experience More at Home:

Go to www.paperplane.org to see designs for some of the fastest paper airplanes in the world. Try some of the designs from 2009 Guinness Book of World Records champion Ken Blackburn.

The Organizer's Checklist for **Paper Airplane**

Station Checklist			
Materials:	Reusable	☐	75-foot roll of black contact paper for the tarmac (this can be used several times; an alternative is to use butcher paper
		☐	Tape measure (to mark distance on the tarmac)
		☐	Chalk (if using contact paper) OR Permanent markers (if using butcher paper)
		☐	Paper airplane templates
		☐	Sheet protectors (optional)
		☐	Sample paper airplanes
		☐	Timer
		☐	Calculator (optional)
		☐	Books about paper airplanes and Bernoulli's principle
		☐	Markers (optional)
	Consumable	☐	Tape
		☐	Copy paper ($8\frac{1}{2}$ x 11 inches) and/or loose-leaf paper ($8\frac{1}{2}$ x 11 inches)
		☐	Chart paper or poster board (optional)
Retailers:	Black contact paper can be ordered online from Amazon (www.amazon.com). It can also be purchased at craft stores or hardware stores. All other materials can be purchased online or from small businesses or large chain retailers.		

Setup Instructions for

Paper Airplane

The Tarmac

1. Attach the tarmac to the floor (use tape to attach butcher paper).
2. Use the tape measure to mark off every 10 feet up to at least 50 feet on the tarmac. Use permanent marker for butcher paper or chalk for contact paper.

Paper Airplane Designs

1. Get paper airplane templates from books or from an Internet search with the keywords "paper airplane."
2. Photocopy paper airplane templates and preserve them in sheet protectors, or laminate them.
3. Use each template to make sample paper airplanes for display.
4. Use the instructions on the Family Fun Card to test the paper airplane designs.

Display

1. Put the Family Fun Card, paper airplane templates, copy paper, timer, calculator (optional), and writing instruments (chalk for contact paper, markers for butcher paper) on display for participants to use.
2. Hang chart paper or poster board for participants to write their names and the distance and/or speed their airplanes flew.

Optional: Provide books about paper airplanes and Bernoulli's principle or computers with Internet access for participants to learn how airplanes fly.

Soapy Boat

Family Fun Card

Which soap is the best "gas" for a boat?

Explore:

1. Use the template to cut out a boat shape from foil, or make a shape of your own.
2. Leave an area for the "gas tank" (a small cutout in the shape of a square) in the back of the boat.
3. Float your boat in a tub of freshwater that does not have any soap in it.
4. Choose the dish soap you want to use as "gas" and use a pipette or cotton swab to place a small drop of it in the "gas tank."
5. What did you see happen? Did the boat move suddenly?
6. Dump out the water and experiment with a different soapy "gas."

Soapy Boat

Family Fun Card

Expected Result:

You should see the boat suddenly move across the water after you put one drop of soap in the "gas tank." One soap may make the boat go faster than another.

Explanation:

Soap spreads easily across water. When the soap in this activity is added to the "gas tank" of the flat foil boat, it desperately tries to escape.

The only place it can escape is through the small slit that leads to the gas tank. The faster the soap can escape through that small slit leading to the gas tank, the faster the boat moves across the water.

Experience More at Home:

Experiment with foil boats that are different shapes and sizes. Discover which brand of dish soap makes the boats you try go the fastest.

The Organizer's Checklist for
Soapy Boat

Station Checklist			
Materials:	Reusable		Scissors
			Soapy boat template (laminate for more durability)
			Plastic or foil pans
			Large empty bin to hold used, soapy water
			Books about boats, floating, or surface tension (optional)
			Test tubes and test tube racks
	Consumable		Foil, cardboard, or another material to make boats
			Dish soap (Dawn and Joy work well)
			Plastic, disposable pipettes or cotton swabs
			Water
			Paper towels
	Safety		MSDS for Dawn or Joy (or other dish soap you chose)
Retailers:	Plastic, disposable pipettes can be purchased from Steve Spangler Science (www.stevespanglerscience.com), Science Bob (www.sciencebob.com), and Amazon (www.amazon.com). They can also be found online by doing an Internet search with keywords "plastic pipette Cartesian." Templates for "soapy boats" can be found by doing an Internet search with keywords "soapy boat." Several designs of flat boats made out of index cards, foil, and cardboard will appear. Material safety data sheets (MSDS) can be found by doing an Internet search using the keywords "MSDS" and the name of the dish soap you chose. For example, "MSDS for Dawn." All other materials can be purchased online or from small businesses or large chain retailers.		

Setup Instructions for Soapy Boat

The Soapy Boat

1. Create templates of flat boats participants can trace or use.
2. If you are designing your own boat, it can have a hull that's triangular, circular, or oval, and the well for drops of soap should be square. Here's an example:

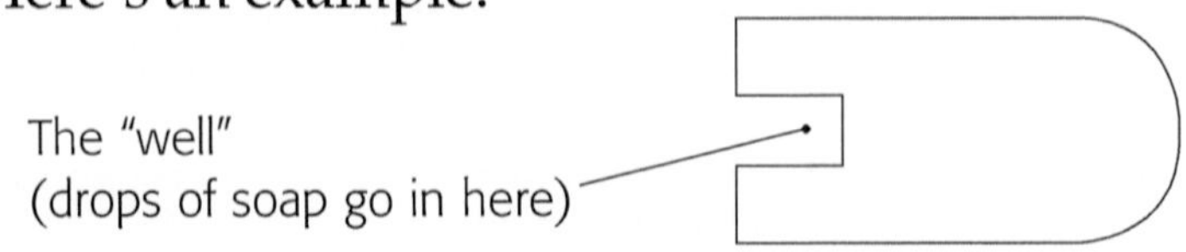

3. Test the boat designs and laminate them so they do not get waterlogged.

The High Seas

1. Get plastic or foil pans and fill them with enough water for the boats to float.
2. Label each test tube with the name of the dish soap.
3. Have a pipette inside or next to each test tube.
4. The boats will need to be tested in clean, soap-free water, so set up a large "Used Soapy Water" bin for used water. Be prepared to dump it often to keep it from overflowing or getting too heavy.

Display

Set out the water-filled pans, Used Soapy Water bin, dish soap–filled test tubes in test tube racks, pipettes or cotton swabs, laminated soapy boat templates, scissors, and boat-making material. Set paper towels off to the side to clean up any water spills. Display the Family Fun Card.

Super Bubble

Family Fun Card

Which bubble recipe makes the taller bubbles?

Explore:

1. Look at the ingredients for the bubble solutions. Which do you think will make the taller bubbles?
2. Step into the center of one of the bubble rings, and grab the large bubble wand.
3. Slowly and gently pull the bubble wand up, up, up ... as high as you can.
4. Step into the center of the second bubble ring and lift the large bubble wand as high as you can.
5. Tell a friend which bubble recipe made the taller bubble.

For a group of three or more people: have one or more people step into the center of the bubble ring.

Super Bubble

Family Fun Card

Expected Result:

You should see a tall, supersize bubble form as you lift the bubble wand out of one of the bubble solutions. The bubble may even go as high as your head!

Experience More at Home:

Glycerin and certain kinds of dish soap are best to make really big bubbles, even bouncy bubbles! Go to www.stevespanglerscience.com/experiment/00000028 to see how you can use glycerin, dish soap, and water to make your own bubble recipe at home!

The Organizer's Checklist for
Super Bubble

Station Checklist			
Materials:	Reusable		At least two inflatable swimming pools
			Carpet squares or towels
			Mop
			Mega Bubble Kit OR Hula hoops
	Consumable		Distilled water
			Glycerin
			Dish soap (Dawn and Joy work well) OR Extreme Bubble Solution
			Large garbage bags (to put wet carpets, towels, inflatable pools, bubble ring, and bubble wand into)
			Paper towels
	Safety		MSDS for Extreme Bubble Solution
			MSDS for Dawn or Joy (or other dish soap you chose)
			MSDS for glycerin
Retailers:	Extreme Bubble Solution and the Mega Bubble Kit can be purchased from Steve Spangler Science (www.stevespanglerscience.com). Glycerin can be purchased from your local pharmacy or large chain retailer. Material safety data sheets (MSDS) can be found by doing an Internet search using the keywords "MSDS for Extreme Bubble Solution," "MSDS for glycerin," and "MSDS" and the name of the dish soap you chose. For example, "MSDS for Dawn." All other materials can be purchased online or from small businesses or large chain retailers.		

Setup Instructions for
Super Bubble

Big Bubble Solution

1. At least 24 hours BEFORE the event, prepare bubble solution (5½ cups distilled water, 5 teaspoons glycerin, 8 teaspoons dish soap)

   OR

   Purchase and prepare Extreme Bubble Solution according to package directions.

Little Bubble Solution

5½ cups distilled water, 4 teaspoons dish soap (use the same dish soap you used for the Big Bubble Solution)

Bubble Wand and Ring

1. Inflate the swimming pool until it is about halfway blown up.
2. Set carpets or towels around the perimeter of the pool so participants can wipe their feet after stepping out of the pool
3. Inflate the large bubble ring from the Mega Bubble Kit according to package directions, if you are using it, and set it inside the ring. Consider inflating the ring only until halfway blown up so it will be as flat as possible. If you are not using the Mega Bubble Kit, skip this step.

4. Connect the large bubble wand from the Mega Bubble Kit according to package directions, and set it inside the inflated ring that is in the swimming pool. If you are using a hula hoop instead, set it inside the inflated pool.
5. Pour the bubble solution into the large inflated ring from the Mega Bubble Kit until it covers the bubble wand. If you are using a hula hoop instead of the Mega Bubble Kit, pour enough bubble solution to cover it.
6. Use your hands to rub the solution all around the bubble wand or hula hoop until it is completely soaked and immersed.
7. Allow the bubble solution to settle into the inflated ring and bubble wand or hula hoop for 30 minutes to an hour. This will give the bubble wand time to completely immerse in the bubble solution and for the inflated bubble ring and pool to settle on the floor.
8. When the event is over, dump the used bubble solution from the bubble ring into the inflated pool. Carry the pool to a sink, a grassy area, or another place that is a safe place to dump the soapy water.

Tip for Super Bubbles

The largest bubbles seem to come after two or three participants use their hands to vigorously rub the solution around the bubble wand from the Mega Bubble Kit and the solution around it becomes foamy.

Display

Have a poster of each bubble recipe set up for families to see. Label one recipe "A" and the other "B." You may also want to have the measured amounts of glycerin and dish soap for each recipe on display, so families can visualize the difference between the two bubble solutions.

Set up the inflated pool, bubble ring, and bubble wand or hula hoop in an area that is OK to have spills. Set the carpet squares or towels close to the pools so participants can step on them as soon as they step out of the pool. Set the Family Fun Card on the table in plain sight for participants.

Super Sand

Family Fun Card

How do hydrophobic things act in water?

Explore:

1. Silane is a chemical people spray on things such as sand to make them hydrophobic, or repellent to water.
2. Try these activities to see how hydrophobic things act in water:
    a. Gently sprinkle a little bit of "Super Sand" on top of the water.
    b. Use the tip of a bottle, a spoon, or another object to gently push the Super Sand just below the water's surface.
    c. See how the sand acts when you push it underwater? How is it the same or different from normal sand?
    d. Stick your hand in the water and try to pull a handful of Super Sand out of the water and put it into the container.
    e. Use a cotton swab to rub a pencil with petroleum jelly. Sprinkle Super Sand on the pencil and dip the pencil into water. What happens to the sand? Tell a friend next to you.

Super Sand

Family Fun Card

Expected Result:

You should be able to see the "Super Sand" form clumps underwater, then become as dry and loose as normal sand when it comes out of the water.

Explanation:

Super Sand is "afraid" of water and is waterproof. This is why it sticks together as soon as it is in water. What makes Super Sand waterproof? A chemical called silicone that has been sprayed on it.

Silicone is the same chemical carmakers spray on windshields so they will be waterproof and water can simply roll off. It is similar to the chemical used in Scotchgard, which keeps clothes from being stained.

Experience More at Home:

Go to www.youtube.com/watch?v=10EnRI80zvk&feature=related to see a YouTube video that explains how Super (also called Magic) Sand works.

Go to ezinearticles.com/?How-to-Make-Your-Own-Imitation-Aqua-Sand&id=4104146 to see how you can make your own Super Sand at home.

The Organizer's Checklist for

Super Sand

Station Checklist			
Materials:	Reusable		Plastic bottle with a squirt tip or nozzle, spoons, or other objects that can be used to push the sand underwater
			Super Sand (sold as Magic Sand or Hydrophobic Sand, or it can be homemade)
			Small plastic containers in which participants can test the sand
			Small plastic containers in which participants can empty tested sand
			Unsharpened pencils
			Can of silane (optional; for display)
	Consumable		Cotton swabs
			Water
			Petroleum jelly
			Paper towels
			Baby wipes
Retailers:	Hydrophobic Sand can be purchased from Science Kit (sciencekit.com). A similar product, Magic Sand, can be purchased from Educational Innovations (www.teachersource.com), Amazon (www.amazon.com), Steve Spangler Science (www.stevespanglerscience.com), or small businesses. All other materials can be purchased online or from small businesses or large chain retailers.		

Setup Instructions for

Super Sand

Super Sand

1. Fill a small plastic container or bowl ¾ full of water. It should have enough water so the bottle with the nozzle tip or the spoon can push the "Super Sand" underwater.
2. Fill the nozzle-tipped bottle with Super Sand, or have a plastic container filled with Super Sand and a spoon ready for participants to use.
3. Have an empty plastic container ready for participants to put the Super Sand into once they remove it from the water.
4. Have paper towels available to wipe up any water spills.
5. Have baby wipes available for participants to wipe the petroleum jelly off the pencils and to wipe their hands clean.
6. Make sure a trash can is available for participants to dispose of their wipes, paper towels, and cotton swabs.

Display

Set the water-filled container, empty container, sand-filled bottle or container with spoon, pencil, cotton swabs, and petroleum jelly on the table together. Set the can of silane (if available) behind those materials so families can see what Super Sand is coated with. Have the paper towels and baby wipes in plain view for participants to use, yet you may want to set out a little bit at a time and refresh the supply as needed. Ensure a trash can is near so participants can dispose of their cotton swabs, wipes, and paper towels. Laminate the Family Fun Card, or display it away from the container of water so it does not get wet.

Wacky Ball

Family Fun Card

Does density make this ball crazy?

Explore:

1. Roll the Wacky Ball to knock the objects down.
2. Roll it in a circle and then in a straight line.
3. Look at both halves of the ball. How do they look the same or different?
4. To understand how the sides of the ball are different, look at and lift both containers in front of you. How is the stuff packed inside them the same or different?
5. What is the connection between the different types of stuff packed in each container and the stuff packed in each side of the Wacky Ball?

Wacky Ball

Family Fun Card

Expected Result:

You should be able to see the Wacky Ball go in large or small circles when you roll it to knock down the objects. It should not roll in a straight line as an ordinary ball would.

You should feel the difference in weight between the containers that are the same size but are filled with two different things of different sizes, which gives them two different densities.

Explanation:

The Wacky Ball has two different sides to it, each with different densities. Density is the amount of stuff you can fit into a certain area. One side of the Wacky Ball has a lot of stuff packed into it and has a high density. The other side does not and has a low density. The side with a lot of stuff in it is not very bouncy. The side that does not have a lot of stuff in it is very bouncy. When the ball is rolled or bounced, each side of the ball acts differently. This is why it cannot go in a straight line.

The Organizer's Checklist for Wacky Ball

Station Checklist			
Materials:	Reusable		Impossiball (a dual-density ball)
			Plastic bowling pins or other objects that are safe to knock down
			Plastic container filled with rice or beans (to represent a dense object)
			Plastic container filled with marshmallows (to represent an object that is not dense)
			Books about density (optional)
	Consumable		Masking tape
Retailers:	Impossiballs can be purchased online from Science Kit (sciencekit.com), Amazon (www.amazon.com), or small businesses. Otherwise, you can do an Internet search using the keywords "dual density impossiball."		

Setup Instructions for
Wacky Ball

The Wacky Ball "Bowling" Area

1. Use masking tape to delineate a straight line on the floor. Use the tape to form an arrow at the end of the line to show the direction in which participants should bowl.
2. At the end of the arrow, set up plastic bowling pins (or other objects that are safe to knock down). The object will be for participants to aim to use the Wacky Ball to knock down the pins.

The "Stuff" Containers

1. Label one plastic container "Dense" and the other "Not Dense."
2. Fill the Dense container with rice or beans and the Not Dense container with marshmallows.
3. Put masking tape around each container so the rice or beans and the marshmallows do not spill.
4. Set up the containers on a table a short distance away from the bowling area.

Display

Display the Family Fun Card, containers filled with rice or beans and with marshmallows, and books about density (optional) on the table. Set up the bowling area a short distance away.

References

Barrow, L. H. (2011, April 22). Organizing a family science night at your school. Retrieved from http://go.hrw.com/resources/go_sc/gen/HSTPR094.PDF

Brenneman, K. (2009). Preschoolers as scientific explorers. *Young Children, 64*(6), 54-60.

Condon, M. (2011, November 9). Science mixes with fun for a great night at Roxbury Township's Jefferson School. *Roxbury Register*. Retrieved from http://newjerseyhills.com/roxbury_register/news/science-night-going-district-wide-in-roxbury/article_2054ea18-0ae1-11e1-81bd-001cc4c002e0.html

Crawford, E. O., Heaton, E., Heslop, K., & Kixmiller, K. (2009). Science learning at home: Involving families. *Young Children, 64*(6), 39–41.

Eberly College of Science, Penn State Science (2011, June 1). Family science night. Retrieved from http://science.psu.edu/outreach/information-for-faculty/family-science-night

Gonzalez-Mena, J. (2007). *Foundations for Early Childhood Education.* Columbus, OH: McGraw-Hill.

Hatton, M., & Sullivan, J. (2011). Methods and strategies: Math and science nights. *Science and Children, 48*(5).

Hochman, D. (2010, September 17). Science night at the coliseum. Retrieved from http://islanders.nhl.com/club/news.htm?id=537813

Sandia National Laboratories. (2011, June 1). Family science night. Retrieved from http://www.sandia.gov/ciim/ASK/documents/fsnsignup.pdf

Stainburn, S. (2011, January 26). How can we reform science education? *The Hechinger Report.* Retrieved from http://hechingerreport.org/content/how-can-we-reform-science-education_4587/

Urban Libraries Council. (2011, April 18). Member Innovations 2010: Family Science Night—Johnson County Library, KS. Retrieved from http://urbanlibraries.org/displaycommon.cfm?an=1&subarticlenbr=364

Walker, J. M. T., Shenker, S., & Hoover-Dempsey, K. V. (2010). Why do parents become involved in their children's education? Implications for school counselors. *Professional School Counseling, 14*(1), 27–41.

Notes:

Notes: